SPECIAL EDUCATION : MUSIC THERAPY

SPECIAL EDUCATION : MUSIC THERAPY

Manorma Sharma

APH PUBLISHING CORPORATION
5, ANSARI ROAD, DARYA GANJ NEW DELHI - 110 002

Published by :

S.B. Nangia
for **APH Publishing Corporation**
5, Ansari Road,
Darya Ganj
New Delhi - 110 002
Tele. : 3274050

ISBN 81-7024-745-4

1996

Typesetting by :
Computer Codes
Virat Bhawan, Comml. Complex,
Mukerjee Nagar, Delhi - 110 009
Phone : 7241200

Printed at :
Efficient Offset Printers,
New Delhi

PREFACE

MUSIC is bestowed upon mankind by Nature for influencing the inner world (spiritual) and moral characters. It is an integral part of social and cultural life of the human beings since it is the strongest form of expression, feelings and is a powerful source of making all-round development in the personality and intelligence of individuals.

Physiological, psychological, physical, moral, intellectual and spiritual effects of music confirm the supremacy of music. Various studies, experiments and empirical researches in India and abroad have established the therapeutic value of music.

The concept of mixing music as a part of therapy on one side with myth, superstition, cult or religion and on the other side questioning about the placebo effects which are faced by every therapy and finally the appeal of scientifically underpinning empirical facts about the concept of music therapy have forced the scientists, musicologists and physicians to put music therapy into action. Music therapy is still in its infancy though it has a long history. Various theories have confirmed the existence of music therapy since times immemorial. Number of agencies are engaged in carrying out research to systematise the form of this therapy. Indian Classical *ragas* have been acclaimed to have healing effects. They stimulate the brain, ease tension and remove fatigue.

Music healing and its refreshing qualities are widely known. The tone, colour and rhythm of seven *swars* match seven *prakriti* (constitution) of human body. These are to be matched for a specific purpose. Thus, it has paved the way to Rag-therapy or music therapy.

Mental retardation is a global concern. The impact of this may range from minor to major disturbances in human behaviour, thought and performance. The neglect, avoidance, rejection, undue criticism, excessive restraints or control and disbelief in the worth and dignity of a child culminates in making him/her a victim of mental deficiency syndrome that adversely affects a child's personality and behaviour. These children are usually substantially below the average child in learning ability and find difficulty in coping with the programme of regular grade levels. To promote their maximum development or to lessen their dependence on society, these mentally deficient children are often provided with programmes of special education. Recently, there has been recognition of the need for special education programme for the mentally retarded children in India. It has been found through a survey that out of the total population of school going children, 25 per cent are below average, on border line and mildly mentally retardates. Thus, the need for special education programmes, whether their purpose be to improve vocational competence, develop potential abilities, or simply improve the quality of living for a group that too often has been condemned to a barren and hopeless kind of existence, provide a challenge that can not be ignored by thoughtful citizens.

Mentally handicapped children meet many obstacles and failures, thus experience feelings of frustration and dejection. They are subjected to maladjustment and deviate from their regular academic requirements. Hence, there is a great need for special education programme. Music education in terms of its potentials for special education has been frequently used as a therapeutic agent. Music education, playing of instruments, listening to music, singing, music performance and active participation are the factors which help in amelioration of the mentally retardates. Particularly, Indian Classical music has been found to be more beneficial in improving the mental state.

The use of music as therapy is based on scientific and clinical approach and has to be used with great care and deep study of the nature of illness. The right type of music selected for such purposes may bring about excellent results whereas the wrong type of music used as therapy may do more harm than good.

The main objective of the author is to provide upto-date information on the mechanism, impact, techniques and strategies to cope with anxiety, stress and mental retardation among children through the use of music as therapy. The concept of music therapy and techniques of using it AS THERAPY, are the main focus of the work. Effect of Indian Classical *ragas* with their multifaceted and multidimensional use pave the way to use Indian Classical music as adjunctive therapy or as a subject of special education for the mentally handicapped children.

The book deals elaborately with the topics of effects of music; mental retardation; amelioration of mental retardation; music therapy, its concept, aims, uses and the techniques of application of music as therapy and in therapy: music as an adjunctive therapy for mentally retarded children and music as a subject of special education. The experimental approach to the subject further enriches the faith in music therapy. It is hoped that this book will prove beneficial for the teachers, parents, counsellors, researchers, musicologists and music therapists.

The success of an academic endevour lies in the active encouragement and support from various scholars and different quarters. It may be difficult to name them but I am indebted to all who made their contribution directly or indirectly. I am specially thankful to the main moving spirit in the entire task, right from its initiation to its completion, Professor A.S. Sethi, Chairman (Retired), Department of Psychology, Himachal Pradesh University, Shimla. I express my gratitude to Dr. M.R. Gautam, former Vice-Chancellor, Indira Kala Sangit Vishvavidyalaya, Khairagarh, for inspiration and, Dr. V.K. Sharma, Senior Horticulturist, Dr. Y.S. Parmar University of Horticulture and Forestry, Solan, who always stood by me with his commitment to academics and concern for quality and excellence.

February, 1995 **Manorma Sharma**

Shimla

CONTENTS

Chapter 1

NATURE OF MUSIC

MUSIC is both an art and a science since it deals with the expression of one's feelings and emotions through sound, in melody and harmony, may be through its composition and execution. On the other hand, it is a science concerned with the systematic management of sound at all levels in the universe. Music term has been used equivocally in a wider sense as symonymous with *sangit* and it has been defined in the Sanskrit texts as follows—

''Gitam, Vadyam tatha Nrityam, tryam sangitamuchyate''

Sangit Ratnakar

"Gitavaditranrityamam trayam sangitamuchyate,
Ganasyatra pradhananatvat tat sangitamitiritam."

Sangit Parijat

According to Sangit Ratnakar, singing, playing musical instruments and dancing are the three components of music while according to Sangit Parijat, singing, playing of musical instruments, dancing are called music but out of these three, singing is the most important. These definitions clearly indicate that music is the combination of the three arts viz. singing (*Geet*), playing of musical instruments (*Vadya*) and dancing (*Nritya*). These three arts are generally referred as fine arts and are closely connected with one another in such a way that it is almost impossible to separate them.

In the study of the Indian music, two major components which have to be understood are— i) the structure of melody, and ii) the structure of rhythm. Melodic structure involves the understanding of various aspects such as the *Nada, Shruti, Swar* and *Raga* etc. The structure of rhythm involves the perception of the *Tala* and the *Laya*.

Objective determinants of music are mainly three elements viz. sound (*Shabda*), tune (*Kala*) and speech (*Vak*). These may be known as material causes or primary material and medium of music. In the Sanskrit language, sound is known as the *Nada*.

Nada

According to the Indian philosophy of *Vedanta*, the word for sound is *Nada Brahma* alias *Shabda Brahma*. Some commentators of the Indian music explain it as *'Nada Eva Brahaman'* meaning, the *Nada* itself is the *Brahma* or the *Nada* is like the *Brahaman*. Further, the NADA is a manifestation of sound which is the sentience (*Sat, Chit* and *Anand*) of the *Brahma*.

Kallinath, the annotator of Sangit Ratnakar, has described the *Nada* as energy of the *Brahma* and the propitiation of the *Nada* leads to the attainment of the *Brahma* which can also lead to the *Moksha* which is the ultimate goal of human life. The *Nada* is the concept of boundless delight i.e. the *Ananda*. It assumes three artistic forms and aesthetic feelings :*Brahma, Vishnu* and *Shiva*, personifying the three supreme powers of the world— creation, preservation and destruction. A single movement called the *Shakti* makes this emanation possible. This energy is also known as the *Nada*.

Matanga Muni has given the principle definition of the *Nada* in Brihaddeshi as follows :

"Na naden vina geetam na naden vina swarah,
Na naden vina nrityam tasmannadatmakam jagat."

There is no song or music without the *Nada*, there are no musical notes without the *Nada*. There is no dance without the *Nada*, the world is filled with the essence of the *Nada*.

Brahma is known to be the form of the *Nada*, so are the Lord Janardana i. e. Vishnu and Maheshwara i.e. Shiva. *Shakti* (power) is also the form of the *Nada*. Air arising from the location of throat (*Kantha*) and moving about up and down, produces the intense course of the *Nada*.

The *Nada* is made up of a dual verbal component. The letter *Na* is spoken of as air and the letter *Da* is known as fire (energy) The word *Nada* is derived from the Sanskrit root *Nadat*— means to make inarticulate sound and it is five-fold viz. *Sukshama* (subtle), *Atisukshama* (very subtle), *Vyakta* (distinct), *Ativyakta* (indistinct) and *Kritrima* (artificial). The subtle *Nada* dwells in naval, very subtle one in the heart, distinct one in the throat, indistinct one in the region of cerebrum and the artificial one in the mouth. Thus, the five-fold placement of the *Nada* be known by wise.

In the chapter '*Swaradhyaya*' in Sangeet Rantakar, Sharangdev has described the indistinct NADA as follows :

"Phalanyudyanti Jeevasya poorvadidalgamina, chakram
Sahasrapatram tu brahamrandhre sudhadharam."

2: 138

"Brahamrandhrasthito jeevah sudhaya sanlupto yada,
Tushto geetadikaryani saprakarshani karyet."

2: 143

"Esham sheshu patreshu chakreshvanyeshu chasthitah,
Jeevogeetadisansidhim na kadachit vapnuyat."

2: 144

The indistinctive *Nada* which dwells in cerebrum or brain (*Brahma Randhra*) is known as *Sahastradalpadama* or *Shunya Chakra* and is the basis of all types of thoughts, virtues and visions. Other *Chakras* are situated in different organs of the body. The *Yogis* (saints) can achieve the *Param-braham* by gaining control over these *Chakras* which can be achieved through *'Geetadi'* (Sangeet) or music.

The term *Nada* as used in Music has been defined by Pandit Sharangdev in Sangeet Ratnakar as follows—

> "Nakaram prananamanam dakaramanalam vidu,
> Jata pranagnisanyogatten nadoabhidhiyate."
>
> 1, 3: 6

The letter *Na* is the indicator of *Prana* (life) and the letter *Da* of *Agni* (energy). With the combination of these letters, the word *Nada* originates. Speech and all the communication of the whole world is dependent on the *Nada* that is why it is said that *Nada* is the supreme power.

The chief and the only property of music is sound or the *Nada*. The Western scientists say that sound is nothing but a sensation caused in the first instance by certain oscillatory motions of the particles of a body, and the effect of these motions being transmitted through some medium, generally atmospheric air, to the ear where they produce impressions on the nerve corresponding to the nature of original motion, causes sound, The Indian music has its deep roots in spirituality and thus, the *Nada* has been explained in terms of musical sound which is of two types— *Ahata Nada* and *Anahata Nada*.

> "Naden vyajyate varnah padam varnatpadavachah,
> Vachso vyavharoyam nadadheenmato jagat."
>
> 1, 2:2

> "Ahatoanahatshcheti dwidha hada nigadyate,
> Soayam prakashte pinde tasmat pindoabhidhiyate".
>
> 1, 2:3

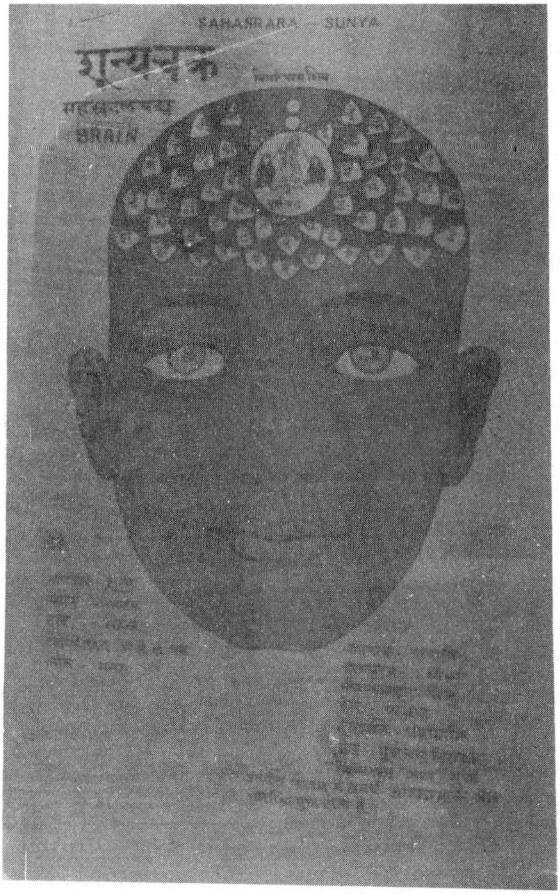

Location of Sahastradalpadam Chakra

The *Nada* is primordial sound and is the very essence of music. The *Nada* manifests the letters (of alphabet), letters constitute the word, and the words make a sentence, so the entire business of life is carried on, through language and, therefore, the whole phenomena i.e. the world is based on the *Nada*.

The *Nada* is said to be two-fold viz. produced and unproduced i.e. *Ahata,* the struck sound and *Anahata,* the unstruck sound. The former being an object of sense perception and the latter a matter of mystic experience of *Yoga* in which sound and light are fused together. The *Nada* manifests itself in the human body and thus, there is direct perception.

The *Ahata Nada* or struck sounds have been classified in Sangit Damodar by Pandit Shubhankar into three groups—Animate sound produced by living beings, inanimate sound produced by lifeless objects and mixed sound produced by human and non-human agencies.

The *Anahata Nada* is the sound which is beyond human experience and it makes a continuous sphere of boundless infinite dimensions.

The *AHATA NADA* can be termed as musical sound. The scientists have given three names to the musical sounds according to their functions i.e. pitch of the sound, intensity of the sound and timbre (character) of the sound.

Immanent sound in the human body is grouped into five types on the basis of its quality of development from the root of the naval to the cerebrum and the buckle cavity of the mouth through the heart and the throat. Matanga Muni and Pandit Sharangdev regard them as shown in the following table :

	Locus	Matanga Muni	Sharangdev
1.	Naval (NABHI)	Subtle	Very subtle (ATISUKSHAM)
2.	Heart (HRIDAYA)	Very subtle	Subtle (SUKSHAM)
3.	Throat (KANTHA)	Manifest (ATIVYAKTA)	Grave (PUSHTA)
4.	Palate (MOORDHA)	Unmanifest (AVYAKTA)	Shrill (APUSHTA)
5.	Mouth (ASYA)	Artificial	Artificial (KRITRIM)

The manifestation of *Ahata Nada* is accounted for by the desire for self-expression. Why there is the desire for self-expression is a metaphysical question which may or may not be answerable. This desire, however, is the cause of speech, and therefore, of singing i. e. music and even dance.

To sum up, the word *Nada* has been used in Indian musicology in the mystical, religious and cosmological senses as well as in the empirical and scientific senses.

Shruti

The word *Shruti* originated from the root (*Dhatu*) *Shru* meaning to hear and thus *Shruti* means any sound that is capable of being distinctly heard by the ear. Authors of treatise of Indian music regards *Shruti* as—

"Nityam geetoyogitvambhishechtvampyut,
Lakshyavidbhi smadishtam pryaptam shrutilakshnam".

It has also been defined by Nanyadev as "*Shruyat Iti Shruti*". Matanga Muni has analyzed the *Shruti* as—

"Shru shravne chasya dhataukti,
Pratyaya smudbhava shruti shabda".

According to him, that which is heard is known as the *Shruti,* it may be one or many. Those who are of the opinion that it is one, they explain that since the *Shruti* is the outcome of the *Nada* which is produced through the combination of bodily fire and air, there is possibility that the *Shruti* is only one. Others accept the *Shruti* to be two-fold because of the division into the *Swar.* Vishvavasu wrote as follows— "Sound itself is known as the *Shruti* on account of being perceived by the sense of hearing. And that *Shruti,* though one, is two-fold according to its division into the *Swar* and the *Antara-swar* i.e. the *Shruti,* situated in the intervals of the *Swar.* Some accept the three-fold *Shruti* on account of its relation with the three *Sthanas* i.e. the *Nada* which is being produced from heart (*Hridya*) known as the *Mandra,* from the throat (*Kantha*) known as the *Madhya* and from head known as the *Tar Sthanas.*

Some authors accept the four-fold *shruti's* divided according to the *Vata, Pitta, Kapha* and *Sannipata.* Tumbru has explained this as "Quality of voice or sound is known by its nature as the high voice that is dry (*Ruksha*) is known as the *Vataj* (originated from *Vata*), the deep, full and clear voice should be known as the *Pittaj* (from *Pitta*), the creamy, soft and sweet voice is the *Kaphaj* (originated from *Kapha*), the voice which combines the qualities of the three types of voices should be known as born of the *Sannipat* (admixture of three)".

Others accept the nine-fold *Shruti's* and this concept is based on the use of the *Swara's* occuring in the holes of the *Venu* (flute). So has also been said by Bharata," the *Swar's* situated in the *Vansh* (flute) should be known as forming groups of two, three and four *Shrutis*". Thus, the number of the SHRUTIS on the flute are nine.

Kohala has said, "some who are adapt in the knowledge of the *Shrutis,* speak of twenty two *Shrutis,* some speak of them as being differentiated into sixty six, others propound their infinity."

Pythagorus is said to have divided the octave into 55 intervals but Euclid of a later period, as a result of some mathematical researches considered a tune or interval into 12 parts. Later, the Greek scale divided the octave into twenty four small intervals.

Though as a matter of fact the *Shrutis* are countless, but, there has been a consensus of opinion since the time of Bharat that they are twenty two in number, who wrote,

> "Vyavhare tvaso tredha hridi mandro abhidhiyate,
> Kanthemadhyo murdhni taro twigunshchotrottrah,
> Tasya dwavinshtirbhedah shravnashrutiyo matah".

It is clear from the above that there are twenty two *Shrutis* which can be distinctly heard. *Shruti* is not only the smallest audible sound but is the accurately audible sound that which is heard in accurate relationship to some other.

Swar

The Sanskrit explanation for note is the *Swar* which is sound, voice, tone in recitation (high or low), accent—*Udatta, An-udatta* and *Swaritta* or a note of the musical scale.

From the micro-tones emerges the seven tones. Tone is analysed in the Indian texts in terms of micro-tones(*Aghata*) and resonance (*Anuranana*) The *Shruti* can correspond to micro-tone of the Western musicology. A micro-tone is an interval smaller than a semi-tone e.g. quarter tone, sixth tone etc. But the Western ears are still not conditioned to make out such fractional intervals within their music.

Abhinav Gupta defines the *Swara* as follows, the sound that is produced by the influence of the sound arising as a result of striking (a vibrating string) as micro-tonal position (*Shrutisthana*) and is thus, essentially resonating, sweet and creamy. Thus on any interval point (*Sthana*) the attacking part (*Abhighata*) of the sound is the *Shruti* and the resonant part the *Swara*.

Similarly, Pandit Sharangdev defines the *Swara* in the following way—Immediately consequent upon the *Shruti*, creamy and resonating, the sound that delights the listener's mind by itself is called the *Swara*.

"Shrutyantarbhavi yah snighdhoanurananatmakah,
Swato ranjayati sarotkritam sah swarah uchyate".

The phrase *Antar-bhavi* is very important. When a string is plucked, the very first sound produced is the *Shruti*, is called the *Swara*, So the *Shruti* is essentially free from resonance where as the *Swara* is characterised by resonance. The *Swara* can also said to be a developed *Shruti*. It is well known to musicologists that the twenty two *Shruti's* in groups of four, three and two go to make the seven *Swaras-sa* (4), *re* (3), *ga* (2), *ma* (4), *pa* (4), *dha* (3) and *ni* (2).

Matang Muni ascertained from the root (*Dhatu*) '*Rajr*' meaning brillance, to which is prefixed the word '*Swa*', so that which means that "which shines by itself", hence, it is known as the SWARA.

"Swayam yo rajate yasmat,
Tasmadesh swarah smritah,"

The *Swara* means the sound which is the progenitor of the *Raga*. The *Swara* is also known as lit, colour or delight.

Similarly, Kohala has also explained that the *Swara* is the delightful sound and it is said to be infinite, on account of its combination with the *Jati*, *Bhasha* (dilaect, language) etc. It is combined with syllabic unit and verse.

It has been generally recognised that it is very difficult to sing this series of 22 *Shrutis* arising one above the other. So, for practical purposes, ancient, mideaval and modern authors and experts in the art and science of music have unanimously accepted twelve principal sounds out of them, and they are known as *Swaras* or notes. The *Swaras* have emanated out of the *Shrutis*. Though the *Swaras* and the *Shrutis* are alike as a matter of sound, yet there is a difference between them, the former being measuring things and the latter, things measured. Indeed the *Shrutis* are to *Swaras* what inches are to feet or minutes to hour.

SWARAS are of 2 kinds—

1. *Shudha*

2. *Vikrita*.

Shudha Swaras are seven in number and are named *Shadaja* (*Sa*), *Rishabha* (*Re*), *Gandhara* (*Ga*), *Madhyama* (*Ma*), *Panchama* (*Pa*), *Dhaivat* (*Dha*) and *Nishạd* (*Ni*). The notes-*Ri*, *Ga*, *Dha*, *Ni*, sometimes become flat or *Komal* when they come downwards from their original place and *Ma* becomes sharp or *Tivra* when it goes higher from flat. Thus, we get five notes in two different forms *Tivra* and *Komal*.

Raga

The term *Raga* is defined in various ways. Some translate it as a tune, others as an air and still others as a melody. None of these definitions, however, give an exact and accurate idea of the Indian word *Raga*.

Raga has been defined in the Indian text as—

'Melodic pattern of tones' (*Swara Sannivesh*).

That which dyes (*Ranjayati Iti Ragah*)

These may easily be analysed and worked to be grouped into the structural and the functional definitions. In the structural sense, it is the most developed tonal form, the stages being micro-tones, tones, simple molecular tones, compound molecular tones, complex molecular tonal motion, mixed molecular tonal motion, finally melodic patterns (*Shruti, Swara, Varna, Alankar, Gamak, Sthaya, Raga* etc.).

In the structural sense, *Raga* means a melodic mode or order of sound or formula, e.g. *Raga Bhairav* is expressed as *Se, Re, Ga, Ma, Pa, Dha, Ni*. In the functional sense, it is to be analysed, as the act of colouring or dyeing (on the part of the maker of music) and interest, joy or delight in a musical note (on the part of the bearer). This is its primary sense and this leads to a wider application of the term. The two senses merge onto the meaning of the word 'melody'. Melody is an apt rendering in English of the word *Raga*.

Bharat used this word *Raga* in compound terms such as *Jati Raga, Gram Raga* at places. And he uses it in the general sense of emotional colour, or aesthetic enjoyment or pleasure. It is Matanga Muni who for the first time used it in the technical sense: "that particular sound (formation) which is embellished by musical tones and the movement of tonal patterns and is thereby delightful to the people's mind, is called *Raga* by wise".

"Yoayam dhvanivisheshstu swar varna vibhushitah,
Ranjko jan chittanam sah ragah kathito budhal".

Matanga Muni had derived the word RAGA from the root '*Raja*', to colour. He brought out the meaning of this derivation grammatically as well as by referring to usage. Kallinath points out that though the word can be derived grammatically as shown above, yet it seems to have acquired a different meaning in usage, such as when one says,"I do not like this *Raga*". The implication of this sort of comment is clear: *Raga* means tonal configuration, more than its literal meaning, the art of colouring (*Rakti*), which refers to its function.

Indian music as already emphasized, is essentially melodic. The music of the folk and the tribes, of religious and sacramental chant and classical art music—all these have the common quality of being based on melody, and ages of experimentation and artistic development of these have given us the concept of *Raga* which is the fundamental basis of the Indian musical tradition.

The *Raga* is a melodic scheme. It is a nucleus based on certain traditionally accepted rules which in actual performance are improvised upon, expanded and embelished, thus, drawing out the possibilities, inherent in the melodic embryo. This simple idea has been made unnecessarily complicated by the pedant. Our music having grown almost totally on the lines of melody, has produced vast varieties of such types of tunes with very subtle differences and it requires an intimate acquaintance with its range to grasp the significance of these subtleties. But the concept of RAGA itself is straight forward and not difficult to understand.

Analogously, a melody is a flow of sound, up and down, with various rhythmic distributions. When we abstract these characteristics and make a type, it becomes a

Raga—musical language. Here again, out of a stream of sound 'notes' are created and named and a particular arrangement of these notes become a *Raga*. The visual representations of such musical symbols is the notation.

Thus, there is a general similarity between language and *Raga*. A *Raga*, then may be defined broadly as a melodic scheme characterised by a definite scale or notes (alphabet), order or sequence of these notes (spelling and syntax), melodic phrases (alphabet), pause and stasis (punctuation) and tonal grace (accent). Of course, there is always a rider, attached to this. A *Raga* must be pleasing, it must have emotional appeal. Therefore, an ancient definition runs, "A *Raga*, the sages say, is a particular form of sound which is adorned with notes and melodic phrases and enchants the hearts of men". As a matter of fact, the word '*Raga*' is derived from the root '*Ranj*' (in the Sanskrit, to please). Further, its general laxical meaning is also emotion, colour and so on.

The *Raga* is a matter of notes. This is just as much true as poetry is a matter of words, or pictures a matter of paint. It is such a long way from being the whole truth that it appears slightly naive if uttered seriously. A *Raga* is also a stringing together of notes in a ripple and a slide and a run of colours. It is an inter-play of feeling an incandescent suggestion of meaning. A *Raga* is all these things and yet is something else. In brief, if given all these things, you have something very much like a *Raga*.

An essential quality of a *Raga* is that every time it is played or sung, it makes a new effect of attention. This attention renewed each time, discovers new words within the known world and opens windows to the horizon. Its possibilities are infinite and yet it always remains unfinished. Its ending is always a temporal ending. This is one reason why a *Raga* can be called the music of the immediate present. In the immediate present, there is no perfection, no consummation, nothing is finished, everything is flying and quivering. It has the quick of both, the past and the future and yet is neither. We can see the invisible in it, laden with mystery and revalation, candidly open in its transit. Uncomposed the *Raga* is on an inculcable pilgrimage of creation. It does not want to get anywhere. It just takes place.

The notes of the *Raga* have little or no meaning on paper: It does not exist until it becomes a part of a person. Here the sequence and the manner in which many items of knowledge about music come to a student is as important as the total pace and subtlity of the relationship between the student and the teacher. The Indian notes-*Sa, Re, Ga, Ma*...etc. as used in the *Ragas* are more than the mere notes struck on a piano. These notes of a *Raga* have a quality which can not be successfully rendered on paper, have very little correspondence to the reality of the *Raga.*

If the *Raga* is, what it is, and this value system on which the music system is based, are what they are, the first order of priority is to obtain an insight into how this music is taught and the nature of the teacher—taught relationship.

Psychological Aspect of Raga

The idea of association of the *Ragas* with season and time of the day does not seem to be as old as the *Raga* system itself. Whereas the *Raga* system begins to have definite form at about the time of Matanga Muni, it is only by the 8th century (Narada's Sangeet Makrand) that such temporal rules are developed. In search of the principles behind the relation of the *Raga* to time, it is necessary to study the ethnopsychological and psycho-acoustical laws and movements that govern musical creation. The other method is to study the immediate responses of the subject to music—psychologically and pasycho-analytically. The responses of the subject can be studied in terms of psychological responses, psychological associations, depth of psychological motives etc. A very useful adjunct to such method is the iconography of the *Ragas*. We have a very rich material, though not always reliable, in the *Ragamala* pictures and the *Raga* descriptions (*Dhyana Murtis*). A psychoacalytical and occultic study would be very fruitful. There is the invariable snake in the *Raga Asawari*, the deer in the *Raga Todi* etc.

In understanding the psychological dynamics of melodic integration, the first necessity is the recognition of the fact that it is the emotional excitement, that is the cause of music, the necessity to communicate with fellow beings, the necessity to relieve deep psychophysiological tensions. This at first appears as an obvious platitude.

The immediate psychological process that motivates musical creation is the emotional tension of the musician (and of course the listener). The musical creation is at once the result of and the relief from such tensions. The tensions at conscious levels are themselves the results or manifestations of deeper infraconscious drives.

Such a psychological state is reflected in the neurophysiological tensions of contractions and relaxations. The acoustical conditions of music, therefore, are the manifestations of such psychophysiological tensions and the desire for consequent adjustments of the organism.

The state of an organism at rest but ready for action is known as the tonus, this is the normal, unexcited state of the neuromuscular system of the organism. Now, a prolonged existence in a tense state is harmful for any organism whichever tries to return to the condition of tonus as soon as the cause of tension is removed, otherwise the organism would become neurotic.

This basic process of organismic behaviour is immediately applicable to musical states of the human organism. Since, musical production is an emotional state, it is necessarily a state of tension. The organism, therefore, always tries to return to a state of tonus from excitation and the resolution of tension to tonus is a very basic process in the neurophysiology of music. The importance of this has been discussed repeatedly in its various aspects, diachronic and synchronic.

It has also been suggested that the cortical activity may also be defined in terms of this tonus. The alpha rhythm in the electro-encephalogram is the usual condition of the brain which is disturbed by certain neuro-muscular activities. This is a fundamental scanning mechanism which, perhaps, is a part of the process of melodic integration or tonal gestalt.

In the light of the above, we may examine the way by which tones are said to have emotional content, for, be it remembered that tones have no emotional value apart from being perceived.

First, the pleasantness or unpleasantness of tones, this is also referred to as the consonance or dissonance value. In spite of the long history behind the study of this question, there is as yet no acceptable knowledge which can give us an insight into the nature of the pleasantness of tones.

To explain consonance-dissonance, Helmholtz put forward the idea of beats; Strunf thought that consonance could be explained by the phenomenon of tonal fusion: Seashore and Melmberg show that at least the mood of the

Raga is partly determined by this factor, particularly with reference to the tonal background due to the drone.

Four factors which they call as smoothness, purity, blending and fusion are necessary for the judgment of pleasantness. Revesz discusses this problem with thoroughness and insight in the light of his own two-component theory and the Gestalt theory. He also points out to the necessity of distinguishing consonance and concordance.

Recently, Ehrenzweig has put forward a very interesting theory of unconscious perception. He has also shown how infra-conscious forces influence our perception of tones, specially what we call tone-colour or tone-quality; this is a very fruitful approach which has to be experimented systematically.

Even taking all this into account, we are not well in possession of all the facts to understand the mechanism of consonance. In the final process, there is resolution of tension due to dissonance into tonus.

Tonal quality or degree of dissonance is, in a sense static. In our music, specially this is perhaps less important than tonal movement. This latter process is even nore complicated than tone quality, for it involves tone quality as well as tonal movements. Here, again the resolution of tension into tonus plays a determining role. The neurophysiology of this resolution has been discussed like this. The departure from the tonic creates a tension which physiologically means the departure from the tonus. The organism will always tend to return to the tonus : the music will, therefore, tend towards pleasant tonal qualities or tonic equipments.

The emotional qualities creatable by such movements are infinite, almost literally so. Particularly, the function of leading tones is important as they create the maximum tension and desire for rest; for the tonic (tonus) is strongly suggestive and called up by them.

One of the guiding principles, we may take the fact that music follows the path of tension resolving. Tones that are constant with one another or the tonic are 'pleasant' and 'restful'. Similarly, tones that move towards the tonic create greater desire for rest and hence create maximum tension: again the *Vakragati* (torturous movement) creates greater tension and confusion than the *Sarala Gati* (linear movement).

The tension which disturbs and confuses the conscious are created by the use of dissonant tones, by the employment of torturous movements and by the avoidance of resting places.

More accurate results can be obtained through the study of three factors—

(*i*) Tonal level,

(*ii*) Tonal quality,

(*iii*) Tonal movement.

Association of tonal level with tones and tonal movements and psychological states should be studied carefully in the laboratory, employing methods of physiological psychology, and general psychology. The theory of numbers and its occultic implications should be taken seriously and worked out.

Creation delight (*Yogananda*), emotive delight (*Bhogananda*) and cognitive delight (*Bodhananda*) can be identified as the aesthetic experience in music.

Rhythm

In music, the time is a vessel through which tone flows. Without time we have no music, just as without space we have no visual arts. From the temporal successions, elementary musical effects and effects of metre and rhythm take place. It is not something external, the different accentuations of beats, which creates musical metre; musical metre is not born in the beats at all, but in the empty intervals between the beats, in the places where time merely elapses. This lapse of time nourishes the rhythmic life of music.

To understand the nature of rhythm in music, one has to see how time is divided, Rhythm is but a particular arrangement of bits of time. Though time is measured by break up of these bits mentally yet we do use outside adjuncts like clapping of hands, beating together of sticks, striking a metal plate or playing on a drum. A very common way of dividing the flow of time familiar to all of us is the ticking of the clock or clapping of hands. All the ticks are uniformly repeated and here we have the simplest breaking of the stream of time.

Rhythm, like melody, has been raised to a high degree of sophistication. Besides the division and distribution of time in the *Tala* and the art of drumming, the compositions and their relation to the *Tala*, the cross rhythms and syncopations in actual performance are further facts of the fascinating but difficult art. So it is said that the first necessity in music is the control of rhythm, for otherwise 'the song and dance will go out of control, like wild elephant without the check of the *Ankush*' (the elephant driver's hook).

> "Talastalpritshthayamiti Dhatordhanji Smrita,
> Geetam Vadyam Tatha Nrityam Yatastale Pratishthitam"
>
> Sangeet Ratankar, ch. 5, 2.

According to Sangeet Ratnakar, singing, playing of instruments and dancing are dependent on the *Tala*. The ultimate basis of everything living or dead, is vibration.

The vibrations when organized and ordered onto manifold creation, i.e. projection designed in a systematic form may be called rhythm. The synonym for rhythm is the *Laya* which is the pace of movement of the *Tala*. It is the speed at which a *Tala* is played. The Indian scholars of music have named rhythm as the *Laya*. It is nothing but a natural harmonious flow of vocal and instrumental sounds and also a regular succession of accents.

B.C. Deva (1967) has described that "the flow of time has to be calibrated. This calibration is called the *Laya* or Tempo. For, if the unit of calibration is large, we feel the passage of time as slow, this is the *Vilambit*. Thus, the *Laya* is the process of calibration of time." Rhythm plays an important role in human life. Regularity is the order of the Nature. The planets move around the Sun in regularity. They also move around their own axis in regularity. Human life, plant life and animal life are bound in their growth and development by strict rules of regularity. Rhythm pattern effects the human mind. The slow motion of rhythm and tempo creates calmness and balanced attitude of mind, whereas fast motions can instil the feelings of bravery, excitement and courage etc. Speed of rhythm is measured through the *Tala* i.e. the *Tala* is a measure of time in music, which is an important factor of every school of music. It regulates the relative duration of musical sounds and as such seems to have considerably engrossed the musician's mind. When accompanying the dance, vocal and instrumental music, the *Tala* maintains the balance which is the most essential character of the Indian music. The *Tala* is independent of melody which if accompanies. It has its own divisions. It moves in bars, (*Khanda*)and each beat in it is divided into small fractions.

The word *Tala* is derived from the Sanskrit root *Tal*. Parshvadeva has defined *Tala* as—

"Tal Shabdasya Nishpatti
Pratishtharthen Dhatuna,
Sa Talah Kalamanam Yat Kriyaya Parikalpitam"

Bharat has described Sangeet as *Swartalspadatamkah*, i.e. a composition which is comprised of the *Swara*, the *Tala* and the *Pada* i.e. tone, metre and verse respectively. The Indian *Tala* or time-measure is more difficult to master than the melody or the *Raga* itself. But since the *Raga* must be sung strictly in the *Tala*, a person cannot know, in any sense, the Indian music until he masters the techniques of the *Tala*. Parshvadeva has outlined the importance of the *Tala* as—

"Talamoolani Geyani Tale Sarvam Pratishthitam,
Talaheenani Geyam Mantrahina Yathahuti."

(Every type of music is dependent on the *Tala*. A rendering of musical composition without *Tala* is like offerings without any hymn—*Mantra*).

In short, the *Laya* and the *Tala* can be understood as the constant interval of time continuously maintained in repeated stress of any kind. *Laya* is thus, a continuous movement in space of time. *Tala* puts a limit to it by dividing the time at a certain desired interval. The constant interval between two ticks of a second is its *Laya*, the minute which measures sixty seconds is the *Tala* (time cycle), while the second is time unit, the *Matra* (beat).

Aesthetic Experiences of Music

Music is a kind of tonal conversation and like verbal conservation, may be simple or compound. Thus provides aesthetic experience. Our own interest is in the combination of the pedagogical and the aesthetical experiences. We are interested primarily in music as a type of particular aesthetic experience. Aesthetic activity may accompany practical, moral, religious, intellectual and social activity and enhance our enjoyment of them. Nevertheless, we can not ignore the relations of musical experience to the other strands in the texture of life. The place music may achieve in a specific curriculum often depends more on the relations of music to other areas of value and life than on aesthetic considerations.

The raw material for musical experience are tones. Each tone has its own qualities of timbre, pitch and loudness. These qualities constitute the sensuous material of music.

We may call these small patterns of tonal material as musical elements because out of them or with them larger patterns are woven. There is a certain level of listening on which one simply hears these elements come and go and responds to them with feelings of pleasantness or unpleasantness. It is something like enjoying the changing colours of a Kaleidoscope. This dramatic change of tensional structure of music may be called its aesthetic form.

It may be noticed that the fine arts are associated with two out of our five senses. These two senses are visual sense and auditory sense. The other senses are so much infatuated with our primordial animal status that there is no scope of aesthetic imagination with those senses such as tactile, olfactory and gustatory senses. But the visual organs and the organs of hearing have led man to artistic and transcendental imagination and to the creation of fine arts.

Fine arts associated with our sense of seeing through the eyes are called visual arts. Such arts are mainly painting, sculpture and architecture. On the other hand, fine arts associated with our sense of hearing are called auditory arts or aural arts. The main aural art is MUSIC.

Dancing in the category of music, is both visual and auditory. It is mainly visual but it requires the accompanying music, vocal or instrumental and so it is auditory also.

The auditory arts on the other hand, are at the same time, time art or temporal art as these arts are to be performed, take some portion of the endless time. The time art is also dynamic art because each and every moment of its performance is transitory. Music as a time art is dynamic in character.

Regarding the essential materials of fine arts, it can be noticed that sound is the basic element of both music and literature. But literature is concerned with the meaning of the words composed of sounds uttered or unuttered, while music is formed only with the sonoric property of sound, the property consisting of pitch, timbre and volume.

Whether in the East or West, all the aestheticians in the field of musical art can be broadly divided into two classes; one holding the view that music is an autonomous world of sonoric beauty having no relationship with worldliness and the other class preaching that music is closely related to all human feelings and the world around us. According to the autonomous school of thought, the essential beauty in music is identified with the sound patterns in progression. The alleged feelings associated with them are somewhere customary, somewhere conventional having no universal groundings and most often fancifully or arbitrarily attributed to the feelings.

Kant, the well known German philosopher and Johann Friedrisch Herbert, not so well known aesthetician, pronounced more distinctly regarding musical aesthetics that—"Music is music and to be beautiful indeed mean nothing."

Eduard Hanslick, the German philosopher, asserted in his work that music can express no indefinite feelings. It has nothing to do with the nature. Natural sounds are quite irrelevant to musical scale. Music originates solely from the fertile imagination of the composer. Its essential beauty is "sound" in motion. Genuine enjoyment of music requires intellectual contemplation of the progressing sonority and a careful guard against emotional outbreak which mars proper intake. Hanslick futher said that though music can not represent any human emotion and feeling, it can, of course represent the dynamic properties of mind—the dynamic aspect, associated with any sort of emotion or feeling. Musical tempo, slow or fast, can be related to mental dynamics. Yet Hanslick seriously warned us, not to correlate music with feelings since the dynamic caused by feelings are far different from the feelings themselves. The dynamic properties of human mind are only concomitant to feelings and never the original feelings. Regarding the beautiful in music, Hanslick finally explained it in a rheotoric language. Music is in his words, 'a vital spark of the divine fire,' Similar is the utterance "*Nada Rupam Param Jyoti*" (Divine fire is Nada) as stated in Sangeet Damodar by Shubhankar.

Plato, the great philosopher, referred to the art of speech and narration before commenting on music. A propagator of the theory of immitation, he suggested that the speaker will have to immitate, for proper effect, claps of thunder, the noise of wind and hails and axles and pulleys, and the notes of trumpets, flutes and pan-pipes and all instruments and even the cries of dogs, sheep and birds. Suitable pitch and rhythm with necessary variations will add to the correct diction and cadence. Speeches and tales must resort to a minimum of such kind of music.

Now, through the dialogues and conversations of Socrates, Glaucon and others, Plato divided the components of song into—i) the words, ii) the tune and iii) the rhythm. As Plato had wanted to do away dirges and lementations in words, so also in song too, he did not require any dirgelike mode of music. This shows that Plato could not indulge in any kind of weakness in human heart.

According to Plato, there should be two fundamental temperaments, i) the swift and energetic and, ii) the slow and mild. Plato, or rather his teacher Socrates did not claim to be expert in music, he rather wanted to disengage his main principle from the specialist's controversy regarding modes of music and their effect. But Glaucon, who was a close associate of Socrates, had sufficient understanding of music, had suggested that the Greek musical modes and the Indian *THATAS* require a separate study.

Apart from the tune, Plato had his fundamental principles on the rhythms which are as follows—

"We must not persue complexity nor great variety in the basic movements, but must observe what are the rhythms of life, that is orderly and brave, and after observing them require the foot and the air to conform to that kind of man's speech and not the speech to the foot and the tune. Of speech the details were left over for Damon's (music experts) consideration." This much Plato asserted that the rhythm and tune should be in accordance with the words and not the reverse.

Nobility and grace, according to Plato, should be the qualities not only of music, but also of painting and similar other craftsmanships like weaving, embroidary, architecture and likewise the manufacture of household furnishings.

Futher, Plato downrightly banished gracefulness, evil rhythm and disharmony in art and society. He condemned the weakness of head which is very often euphemistically styled as goodness of heart.

Socrates and Plato alongwith Glaucon wanted to introduce music education in the State. According to them, "education in music is most sovereign because more than anything else, rhythm and harmony find their way to the inmost soul and take strongest hold upon it, bringing with them and imparting grace, if one is rightly trained."

Futhermore, Plato commented that a true musician must be able to recognise the form of soberness, courage, liberality high-mindedness and all their kindered opposites, and all the combinations that contain and covey them neither in trifles nor in great things but believing the knowledge of them to belong to the same art and discipline. On the whole music should bring forth a coincidence of a beautiful disposition in the soul and corresponding and harmonious beauties of the same type in the bodily form.

The next contention of Plato is that music and beauty lead to the philosophy of love as opposed to extravagant pleasure which leads to ultimate pain. The consumation of music culture is the love of the beautiful.

Aristotle also pleads for music education as it is in harmony with human soul. Melodies and rhythms contain representations of anger and wildness, courage and temperance and all other moral qualities. Musical expression most closely correspond to the true nature of these qualities, to the true character and soul. There can be diverse kinds of melodies which produce diverse types of affections. Aristotle quoted some examples, such as Mixolydian makes men mournful and restrained, while the Plerygian makes men enthusiastic and the Dorian is always ethical. The rthyms also have the similar power. Some of the rhythms are of stable character while some others are of emotional nature, and of the latter some are vulgar, connected with cheap wish which are always avoidable in education.

Aesthetician Kant says that art of tone, that is, music, expresses itself by means of sensation without concepts and leaves behind no food for reflection of thoughts. Still music moves the mind more diverseiy. Inspite of being transient, it has an intenser effect. In his view, music is more a matter of enjoyment than of culture. Its effect is caused by a more or less mechanical association. He also thinks that music is a language, a language of the affections through the law of association. But the aesthetic ideas inherent in a piece of music are not concepts or determinate thoughts. The form of the arrangement of musical sensations comprising harmony and melody expresses the aesthetic idea of an integral whole of an unspeakable wealth of human self and that, sonorous wealth itself is the affection in a piece. Thereafter, it is a matter of taste which constitutes the judgement of an individual.

Hegel thinks that music is a romantic art and no kind of objectivity enters into its sensuous element, that is sonorious sound, in its mode of expression and communication. Musical elements are ever passing and unstable in character as these arise and vanish in the ether. This kind of obliteration makes music romantic. The form and content of music are subjective in character and communicate the inner life. The sensuous material in music vibrates in itself and always is in movement. This vibration and dynamism constitute the life and spirit of music.

Music relinquishes and obliterates the external form of perceptible visibility. According to Hegel, music can express the object-free inner life or the abstract subjectivity. The chief task of music consists in making resound, not the objective world itself, but on the contrary, the manner in which the inmost self is moved to the depths of its personality and conscious soul. The effect of music is also the same. It directly addresses the soul. Pure music leads us to object-free inwardness.

Music may be regarded as a universal language though the character of note-formation differs from culture to culture. The effect of music, according to Hegel, proceeds not to the intellectual realm but to the movement of heart and inner self in a abstract way. Music, in accordance with the quality of its content form, and simultaneously in accordance with the aptitude and temprament of the listener, may have varied kinds of effects such as emotional, sensuous, melodious, harmonic, rhythmic, erotic, joyous, intellectual, pangfull, devotional, patriotic and so on. Yet the peculiar power of music is elemental.

Music fills the void of a particular duration of time. It involves the subjective feeling both of the performer and the listener and thereby acquires a subjective unity.

According to Hegel, as single note may be animated by feeling and become the expression of it. But music as a whole is constituted by the relationship and inter-connection of notes—the relationship of succession in melody and that of concordance in harmony. Fragmentary notes may have their sources in Nature but artistic relationship is the achievement of art.

Hegel is a sincere admirer of the vocal music and according to his observations and likings, the human voice is the freest and the most perfect instrument which unites in itself the qualities of both wind and string instruments because in the human voice a column of air vibrates for note production and through the vocal muscles, there comes to play the principle of tightly stretched strings. Consequently the musical voice can be perfectly synchronized with both wind and string instruments. Besides, this the human voice is the direct expression of the soul itself. Of course, the voice must be made so perfect as to produce the perfect note without any kind of unwanted noise.

Melody, according to Schopenhauer, has significant internal connection from beginning to end. Melody records the secret history of human feelings and passions. Human will strives, is satisfied and strives again. Human passions move from wish to satisfaction, from satisfaction to newer wishes and so on. Melody expresses such multifarious efforts of will. Satisfaction is expressed by return to the key-note. Tension of mind or languor is expressed by a delay of this return. Quick melodies depict cheerful moods and sadness can be depicted by slow ones. Quick dance music represents only the easily attained shallow pleasures. The change of half a tone e.g. the use of the minor third instead of the major, can produce an anxious feeling. Thus, there are infinite possibilities of melodies corresponding to inexhaustible transitions of human will.

Further, according to him, music is a universal language and its universality is not of abstraction but of definiteness. It resembles geometrical figures which are universal, definite and perceptible forms of various possible objects of experiences. This is also an analogy only to express certain inherent truth. In short, music exhibits itself, 'as the metaphysical to everything physical in the world, and the thing in itself to every phenomenon.'

All possible music deviates from perfect purity. The equally tempered scale is artificial to some extent and it has been attained through age old trial and error of the placement of notes. Every system of scale formation has to try hard to conceal the discords. 'A complete, pure harmonious system of tones is not only physically but arithmetically impossible. Yet, even through this imperfect system, music achieves its highest results.' It is similarly possible in human life also.

The metaphysical side of music is not arbitrary. It has rather a sound basis to the physical aspect of music. All the notes of the octave have a rational relation to one another. The said relation depends on their respective vibrations. Coincidence of vibrations produces consonance, as opposed to dissonance resulted from irrational relation of vibration.

Rhythm comes from the relative duration of the notes and pitch depends on the relative rapidity of the vibrations of the notes.

Herbert Spencer formed an obvious hypothesis set forth on the principles of psychology that music being one of the faculties of human nature, its root must have remained in his pre-existing archaic elements. Muscular contractions of our vocal organ, caused from diverse sensations, emotions and passions, affect our voice in the forms of fluctuation of pitch, timbre and volume and also in the degree of rapidity and slowness of tones emitted in the automatic and continuing succession during vocal rendering. Music is a development of this tonal element or our vocal expression.

Arising out of passions corresponding to muscular stimuli, music attains its developed art form by virtue of aesthetic endeavour of the composers through their refined sensibilities. The technicalities conform to the grammar only while the spirit of music is directly corresponding to the inner sensuousness of the musician.

Spencer has pronounced a pragmatic theory regarding the formation of music. Immediate pleasure should never be the end of music. Musical effect transcends mere enjoyment. The delights of music obviously ministers to the welfare of individual and society. Music not only originates from feelings but affects feelings of the listeners. As words are the 'Signs of ideas' tones and tunes are the 'Signs of feelings'. The feelings associated with beautiful music are not always gross and familiar as found in the music of the savages, but refined and apparently unfamiliar in our day-to day life. Therefore, the function of music is to facilitate the refined development of our feelings, emotions and passions. Music should be regarded, according to Spencer, as an aid to the achievement of a "higher happiness" of an unexperienced falicity of" an unknown ideal life."

Tagore has strongly suggested that music is not only a conglomeration of notes and rhythms but the main purpose of the music should be the expression of human feelings such as joy, sorrow, surprise, anger and all other sundry emotions.

Indian music in general and particularly, the musical culture have evolved and advanced immensely in course of time. Aesthetic awareness has surcharged to-day's performance. Music lovers of the present era are aware of the fact that dry grammar can not make an artist. Immitation and pedagogy have been replaced by genuine creativity. Our music is mere combination of notes. Until we instil feelings into it, we can not be proud of our musical culture. Apart from this music and dance alongwith other arts are being regarded as means to the welfare of humanity and not for temporary entertainment only.

Music is defined in terms of seven variables—medium (tonality, timbre), form, content, maker, making and realization, and chromatic fusion of all these becomes an instance of music with the actual values of the variables. They include the relations of tonal patterns of musical diction to the emotive stereotypes and turn these into aesthetic stereotypes by virtue of their property, organic unity, deterrents, opposition and harmony among themselves and other aesthetic properties. These in their tonal effects make the music more or less musical. And then not only can two musical acts be comparable, the phenominology gradation of the seven variables becomes logically justified. Music affects the brain through the ears. It first pleases the ears, then stimulates and refreshes the brain with its sweet concord. Rhythm and melody find their way direct to the secret recesses of the soul. There is no other science than these fine arts which can make man, milder, gentle, better behaved and more reasonable. Music is the most valuable means of upbringing the youth, it eliminates wilfulness, impropriety and coarseness from human thoughts and action. It adds on the other hand, firmeess, moderation and harmony to the character and leads ultimately to happiness. Music strengthens mind through concentration of will force through the medium of sweet and beautiful combination of musical notes.

The concept of music therapy has emerged from the correct intonation and right use of the basic elements of music such as the *Nada, Shruti. Swara, Raga, Tala* and *Laya*. Of course, what has been said is only about the technicalities of music. But a land which has had millions of civilizations, a fantastic variety of cultures and geographic distribution of great immensity presents a multitude of social and cultural problems related to music. A study of these problems gives the necessary background for understanding the present. So the history, social relations, aesthetic attitude and such matters will have to be discussed.

Chapter 2

MUSIC AND ITS EFFECTS

MUSIC is bestowed upon mankind by Nature for influencing the inner world (spiritual) and moral characters. It is the art of combining sounds for reproduction by voice or by various kinds of musical instruments, in rhythmic, melodic and harmonic form to express thought or feeling. According to Webster's New Collegiate Dictionary, "Music is the science or art of incorporating intelligible combination of tones into composition having structure and continuity."

Since the dawn of civilization, music has been an integral part of social and cultural life of the human beings. Music in one guise or another permeates every human society. Throughout history, music has been an important adjunct to ritual and drama and has been credited with a capacity to reflect and influence the human emotions. Various musicologists and psychologists have acknowledged that music is a powerful source of making all-round development in the personality and intelligence of human beings.

Music is the oldest form of expression, older than language or art; it begins with the voice and with our overwhelming need to reach out to others. In fact, music is far more than words, for words are abstract symbols which convey factual meaning. Music touches our feelings more deeply than most words and makes us respond with our whole being. The combination of music and speech into single expression of song has unique power, conveying feelings of great elation or almost unbearable poignancy.

When we gather for common celebrations, music helps to raise the sharing of feelings to a level of intensity which words alone could not hope to attain. Music does not produce the world outside and around us, not even when we consciously initiate the sounds we hear; music is first and foremost about us, it is our identity. Every ritual we share, calls for its own music: birth, marriage, death, and planting and harvesting a crop, the change of seasons, the coming of spring, the sufferings of illness and recovery of health.

In Indian tradition, the 'OM' is the primary cosmic sound energy that created the entire universe. This is described as a humming sound (Anahat Nada) that saints are able to hear during meditation. The 'VAK' or human speech is a manifestation of *Saraswati* in our culture. The many legends about saints *(Rishis)* pronouncing a curse or benediction which would become a factual event, show the great belief in the power of human sound. The Vedic chants were intoned with utmost care as each intonation and inflection of the voice could have beneficial or adverse effects. There was a great but powerful belief in the power of sound among our forefathers and so our mythological stories are full of legends that affirm their faith. Our Gods are also closely associated with music, it is believed that the five primary *Ragas* of the Indian Classical Music owe their origin to Lord *Shiva* while the sixth one to Goddess *Paravati*. *Saraswati*, the Goddess of learning and music is always shown with the Veena. The charismatic effects of Lord *Krishna's* flute are well known. Spiritual music frees us from our baser self, speaks to us of man at peace with himself and God. It reflects the rhythm of a society which has established its faith and security. This is music standing on the pinnacles of human discovery and invention. Music is a mirror of the process of thought itself. The repeated rhythms and sequences of tones clearly helped to establish the principle of recognition and comparison, drawing on memory and on trial and error.

All the various symbolic methods we use to investigate the nature of the world and ourselves are to be found within music.

We seek knowledge, in order to gain control over the unpredictable, for in all of us, there is a psychological need for reassurance, if we are to create order and sense out of events, to give them focus and direction. Any one cell may become ten million, giving its genes to its offspring, and thereby establishing the repetition of the genetic pattern. With man the process of conscious as well as psychological.; we depend on the products of our minds and hearts, and among these is music. Just as the involuntary heartbeat produces life's first rhythm, so music gives back to us the pulse of life. Music has been created for the building of a society for the harmonious blending of the spiritual and mental set-up of all people and is thus, an integral part of personal life of the human beings.

General Effects

Effect of music in different forms on every aspect of human life, plants, animals and even non-living things has been studied. In ancient mythology, Lord Hanuman is said to have melted rocks with the rendering of particular *Raga*. The compelling charm of Lord Krishna's flute is also legendary. Historically, we have the legends about Tansen, creating a raging fire by singing the *Deepak Raga*. Dikshitar invoked rain on the porched countryside by rendering *Amritvarshini Raga*. We can not be sure how much all this is fact, but the fact that people believe in the dynamic power of music is proved by the popularity of such tales.

Physiological Effects

Music increases the metabolic activities within the human body: it accelerates the respiration, influences the internal scretions, improves the muscular activities and as such affects the nervous and circulatory systems of the listener and the performer. Singing organizes the individual's vocal apparatus, improves speech and develops vocal-auditory co-ordination. Farnsworth (1967) stated that music may bring physiological changes. He found significant reduction in the fatigue, and a stimulation to the depressed feelings among the mentally and physically handicapped persons when they were subjected to music listening and participation. Pathak (1969) while discussing the effect of music as a means of relieving tension suggested that music can reduce tension of nerves and so the listener feels happy, courageous and energetic. Klitz (1970) suggested that participation in musical activities encourages better posture and proper breathing and strengthens specific muscle groups, removing frustration and reducing emotional tensions.

Music can develop the individual's response system to the impact of sound. There are basically two ways to consider the impact of music of human beings on biological development of human beings on biological development, 1) loud music arouses as indicated by elevated pulse rate, muscle tonus, blood pressure , blood glucose levels etc. 2) rhythmic, soft and familiar music produces opposite physiological responses as it relaxes the tension and at times can lead to sleep; it relieves hypertension.

Functioning of different organs within the human body is affected by music and it has definitely a regulatory effect on physiological processes such as digestion, blood circulation, metabolism etc. Actually rhythm enhances muscular tonus and most likely creates a desire for physical activity. Our bodies are capable of following music to a remarkable extent that promotes growth and physical fitness. It is a fact that structure and functions of the human body are maintained through exercise, without which it degenerates the functioning of human body system. Speaking from physiological point of view, activities like playing the music, primarily drums and other rhythmic exercises enrich the speed of motor responses by enhancing the speed of signal transmission along nerve fibres and in terms of bio-chemical functioning, this activity increases the individual's ability to liberate free fatty acids from its fat deposits to fuel muscular work.

Psychological Effects

Among the psychological effects of music, the most pronounced ones are on the behaviour and temperament of the individual. Emotions, feelings and thoughts have been reported to be greatly influenced by music listening or participation. Joy is born both in the process of actively participating in music making and in the process of listening to it. Emotional experience derived from music has a powerful effect on the formation of one's moral and intellectual outlook. Music activities lead to development of imagination and creative thinking. Singing, playing a musical instrument or rhythmic movements provide better sense of proportion, a finer perception and a happier world outlook. Shyness, aggressiveness and many other such characters of individuals have been normalized by music. Mere humming of musical tones may enable a person to overcome loneliness. Music has a great ability to inspire and enthuse the listener and the performer. Thus, it is used as an important and forceful weapon for arousing the will power of the army.

Schopenhauer (1883) observed that the effect of music is strong, quick, necessary and infallible on the emotions of human beings. Desirable effects of music have been described by Copland (1952) as "it can stimulate or sooth the mind, help towards a wider education or, at least, a wider mental perspective, can gently plough the mind to be more receptive to learning, desciplined physical action, comfort the lonely and the sick, awake pleasant memories in the old, delight the young, and lull the child to sleep."

Sledzinski (1970) had outlined the role of art including music in the life of man and found that it shapes integrity, moulds feelings and imagination, induces creative abilities and enables to overcome loneliness, boredom and discouragement among the individuals. It has been reported by Attri (1981) that every living being is affected by music which may or may not be assessed immediately as its effect is though slow but is long-lasting on the feelings, mood, emotions and behaviour of both the applicator and the receptor. Goswami (1977) observed that all the three states of mind i.e. conscious, sub-conscious and unconscious, are involved during the process of learning music by an individual. Conscious mind is at work during learning and then the learnt piece of music goes to the sub-conscious mind which is then passed on to the unconscious mind. Conscious and sub-conscious mind may become inactive due to high frequency of unconsciousness and as the consciouness may be lost and the affected person behaves in an abnormal way which causes mental disturbance, mental depression and mental retardness. Their cure or improvement is possible through music. She further reported that music is the sound expressed as feelings, even before the discovery of any script or language.

According to Thanvi (1982) music has limitless effects on human beings and it affects their mental behaviour. She had also observed that mind is very closely related to music. Due to this fact, attempts have been made with the help of music to improve the behavior of the individual from the ancient times. Klara Kokas (1966) used Kodaly's method of music instruction and observed that music education crossed the boundaries of music itself in its influence and became a more effective means of moulding the personality of children than could have been expected. Slack (1970) studied the effect of music education on the slow learner pupils and found that music education had a positive psychological effects in the normalizations of their pent-up emotions and developed their abilities to the full. Klitz (1970) observed that music education brought about the sense of accomplishment, recognition and gratification. It generated enthusiasm, instil confidence and motivated them to seek additional knowledge of music. A number of mentally retarded children showed dramatic behavioural changes as a result of their participation in music programmes.

Elord (1972) tested and compared the effects of participation in a combined perceptual -motor and music programme with a music programme to study the effects on perceptual motor skills, general behaviour as observed in classroom behaviour, personal health habits, physical education participation and social adjustment. Comparing two groups of 15 educable mentally retarded children , he concluded that a combined perceptual-motor and music programme will develop perceptual motor skills to a much greater degree than music programme alone but the similar gains will be made in social and emotional behaviour in either a combined programme or a programme in music alone.

Doron Kemp Antrin says, "Psychologists have found that music does things to you, whether you like it or not. Fast tempos invariably raise your pulse rate of, respiration and blood pressure; slow music lowers them," This quotation depicts the tremendous beauty of the influence of music on human physiology and psychology. Music acts to dull pain (mental) and put or transform a person into a mild trans. Thus, music has tremendous impact on human biology. In certain cases children deprived of parental affection or proper home environment are obsessed with the power of music. William Green says "Music is a friend of labour, it lightens the task by refreshing nerves and spirit."

Physical Effects

Music may directly or indirectly affect the physical changes in an individual. Exercises done in music provide the individual with a good posture and improves his motor coordination. It also improves his walking and running habits . Aerobic exercises combined with music are the good examples of these effects. Apart from these, expression of joy, happiness and other feelings which appear on the face during participation in music either as listening to or making music, brings indirect physical changes in the individual. It is the inherent nature of man that at the time of fear or anxiety, he feels secure by hearing or playing music. In situations of depression, he feels a great relief by hearing or playing music. Sound has a marked but immediate effect on the physiology of the body. The regular motion of the heart and lungs reinforces the sense of rhythm. And , dance is but the response of the body as a whole to the natural instinct of the rhythm. Similarly, the gradual development of the vocal acts originally involves the intellectual correlation of behaviour just as any other physiological process.

Specific types of music can correct certain physical disorders. Blowing the horn improves abdominal muscle weakness while playing on the cello improves the correction of polio. It has been observed that there was improvement in a polio victim since it helped in the better finger coordination. It is also recommended for patients suffering from cerebral palsy. Cripples develop better coordination of limbs by moving and doing exercises with music. In geriatrics, old people have a better morale and suffer less from boredom and loneliness. A study carried on stammering in children with the use of music, has shown that insufficient breathing, over excitement, self-consciousness, inferiority complex and lack of coordination of psycho-neuro muscular mechanism are the causes of stammering. The use of right type of music in such cases and the use of participation techniques in music, simple rhymes and tunes have been found to facilitate the cure of stammering. Hence it is emphasised that music which has a tremendous impact on human biology is most adaptive.

Prenatal Effects

Amazing diversities of tone justifies the claim that the effects of music have been experienced since the onset of humanity. From ontogeny it is known that a foetus is sensitive to stimuli from the sixth month on and reacts to perceptions. It senses the mother's heart-beat, respiration and intestinal sound via' vibration hearing', a combination of mechanical and tacticle stimuli transmitted through the amniotic fluid. Other messages are conveyed by mother's voice. The swing of her body while walking, of external noises that a foetus participates in the tonal events or situational emotions, is a fact well known to female musicians who are often unable to continue in their profession during the last three months of pregnancy because of their offspring's too vigorous expressions of pleasure or displeasure.

Some of our ancient beliefs are strongly supported by modern scientific discoveries. Abhimanyu, the son of Arjuna while he was still in his mother's womb, is said to have listened to the first phase i.e. how to fight in the "Chakravyuha" which was complex formation in warfare. Later, her mother fell asleep so he could not listen the remaining part as how to come out of the "Chakravyuha". After birth, as an adult, when he entered the 'Chakravyuha', was not able to come out, so was killed. 'Ashtavakra' who is the author of 'Ashtavakra Gita', is said, got eight deformities of his limbs because he had heard the

Vedas recited wrongly eight times while he was still a foetus. In support of these views, recent researches have established that the sense of hearing is the only sense that develops even before the birth of the baby and the baby is capable of absorbing knowledge conveyed through sound while in womb.

The soothing effect of right tunes is evident when we look at lullabies. These are simple tunes and rhythms which instil the child to sleep. The main technique or effect of these lullabies is that of repetition which has a sedative effect. Here the quality of voice or expertise in singing is not as important as the familarity of the voice and music. The child feels secure and reassured by hearing the familiar voice of his mother even though it may be a cracked voice.

Moral Values of Music

Music has been acredited with moral values from the ancient times. For Aristotle, music could be' a stimulus for goodness, capable of having an effect on the character, and so capable of forming men who have the habit of right critical appreciating and contributing to intelligent and cultivated pastime.' Plato also believed strongly in the moral values of good music: he says "for rhythm and harmony penetrates deeply into the mind and have also a most powerful effect on it, and if music education is good, it will bring balance and fairness."

Chinese and Greeks both have equated music with morality. Confucius, around 500 B.C., wrote "Character is the backbone of our human culture . Music is the flowering of character." Tolerance, love and social harmony are the by-products of an artist's way of life and creation. Beauty and truth, two great disciplines when combined, as they are in music, where order is based on self-restraint and a better understanding of repose, will lead to greater maturity, awareness and equilibrium in our civilization. Words may conceal truth but this is hardly possible in the case of music, even when it is used corruptly. We should be able to detect the unwholesomeness within, if we listen with care. In any event ,it is the musician's role to maintain our trust in the world, and the world's trust in us, to help us express genuine emotions. When music takes on that responsibility, it draws upon the best kind of human effort and is deeply therapeutic, harmonizing the physical, the spiritual, the intellectual and the emotional, joining body and the soul. Moreover, instruments producing music under human guidance were considered to be a link to the divine and eternal BRAHMA. Naturally, musical objects were preserved in a society where tradition and ancestoral worship played a crucial role. Szabo (1970) working in Hungary, reported that singing opens the door to a broader knowledge of music of all, Singing in a group, is an effective means of moulding character as this evokes feelings of joy, and feelings of fellowships difficult to express in words, and the feelings expressed after a successful group performance shows satisfaction, pleasure and contentment.

Sokolov (1970) working in the U S S R reported that choir singing, besides helping to breed feelings like patriotism, civic responsibilities and collectivism also help to strengthen the friendship of world growth and sense to acquire moral characters. Maudgalya (1980) found that community singing has a very important role to play at every level. It would be a far more helpful and successful media for developing a sense of discipline, unity, love and respect for other languages and religion.

Effect on Animals

Investigators have also studied the effect of music on animals. Effect of music on animals like camel, horse, snake, hippopotamus, rhinoceros and milch animals, particularly, the cows have been studied both by musicologists and scientists. It is said that Lord Krishna used his flute to attract the cows and then to encourage their milch yielding capacity. It has been scientifically proved that cows yield more milk when they are milked white music is played.

It has been reported by Tiwari (1980) that Pandit Onkar Nath Thakur studied the effect of music by rendering of the *Raga Bhairavi* on violin on a fierce lion in a zoo. It was found that the lion lost his fiercefulness and became normal as a result of the effect of the *Raga Bhairavi.* Horses and camels when moving in a column in the army or elsewhere have been found to be more disciplined while the music is being played.

Considering from the point of view of bird pest management, certain experiments have been conducted at the All India Co-ordinated Centre for Bird Pest Management at the Andhra Predesh Agricultural University Campus, Hyderabad. The distress calls of the birds when played on the tape recorder in the field resulted in scaring the birds away from the field, as such protecting the crop from the damage to be done by the birds. Distressed calls of the birds as parakreet, crow and some animals like jackals, pigs etc. have been tried to scare away the birds and animals from the fields and orchards and much success has been reported.

Effect on Plants

Similarly, the effect of music, on the plants has been studied, Growth of plants has been reported to have increased under the influence of music. Quality and quantity of the produce have been significantly affected by music.

Thakur (1981) reported that Dr. T.C.N. Singh of the Botany Department of Annamalai University has successfully demonstrated an increase in the yield of rice crop as a result of music application. Apart from this, increase in the yield of peas, sarson and beans has also been reported by him. '*Behari Raga*' played on violin has been found to be most effective.

Other Effects

There are references in literature which indicate the effect of different types of music, particularly Indian Ragas on the surroundings: '*Raga Deepak*' may cause fire while '*Raga Megh*' and '*Raga Malhar*' may bring rain. There are also reports that music can calm storms and increase the fertility of soil.

Mental Therapy

Music has been employed as a therapeutical tool for correction of various physical disorders and emotional disturbances.

Music and other arts were frequently used as the therapeutical agent in ancient societies. One of the most famous example is contained in a passage from the Old Testament, "And it came to pass, even the evil spirit from God was upon Saul that David took the harp, and played with his hand; so Saul found relief, and it was well with him, and the evil spirit departed from him." (1 Samuel, 16 : 23)

Indian classical music and folk music have been found to have direct and long lasting effects on various aspects. Indian classical music is the traditional music which is based on systematic sequence of musical notes. It includes a number of Ragas and each Raga has its own specific effect on the emotions of the listener and the participant.

Many investigators have studied the effect of different Ragas on human beings and animals and have confirmed the fact that they leave a long lasting effect on the listener.

Classical music is the basis of all types of music. Rendering of the *Raga* involves both physical and physiological participation of the performer. The sounds so produced in various forms originate from the inner parts of the body, particularly the heart and the throat. This involves physical as well as metabolic changes within the body. Muscular, circulatory and nervous systems are directly involved in the participation i.e. rendering of different *Ragas*. Various facial expressions, gestures, and body movements, especially of arms and hands, during the performance of a *Raga* depict the thought, feelings and emotions of performer and the listeners.

Some work has been carried out at the M.S. University, Baroda, India, for the correction of aggressiveness, heart ailments, mentally disturbed persons, mentally depressed and slow learners, with the help of music, Beneficial effects of various *Ragas* like *Bihag, Kafi, Malkauns, Ramkali, Hindole, Bahar, Deshkar, Lalit* and *Jaijaiwanti* were observed since the conditions of such persons showed some improvement (Bhattacharya, 1970). Pandit Onkar Nath Thakur, as reported by Tiwari (1980) had observed number of beneficial effects on human beings. A boy suffering from insomania was cured as a result of the rendering of *Raga Puriya* by Pandit Ji. It has been reported by Ved Mani Singh Thakur (1981) that malaria, hysteria, insomania, tuberculosis, constipation, typhoid and many other diseases can be cured through various Ragas like *Hindole, Marwa, Puriya, Bilawal, Tilang, Ramkali, Multani, Kalingra, Sohni, Paraj, Todi, Bhairavi, Malkauns, Piloo, Bihag, Darbari Kanhara, Khamaj, Sorath, Adana, Megh Malhar, Asawari, Bhairav, Vrindavani Sarang, Desh* etc.

These *Ragas* embrace a wide variety of emotional content. They can be courageous, amorous, meloncholy, cheerful, soothing or ecstatic in their effect and are capable of conveying these qualities to the listener. Some melody types are supposed to influence the illness, calm storms, tame wild animals and increase the fertility of the soil. Significant increase in the growth of plants, yield of milch cattle and cure of many physical ailments and diseases has been a worldwide known fact : *Ragas* have pernicious power. For example a certain Raga may cause fire (The New Encyclopaedia Britannica Knowledge in Depth, Vol.IX, 1973-74).

Deva and Vermani (1968) conducted an exploratory study using Indian classical music *(Ragas* like *Kafi, Misra Mand, Puriya Dhanashri* and *Rageshwari)* and improvised psychological research tools to study the psychological response of Indian listeners. All these *Ragas* exhibited significant response from the listeners Therefore, they suggested that there is great scope for conducting extensive research in this field.

Altekar (1968) observed that *Ragas* like *Shankara, Patdeep, Hindole* and others have proved beneficial in bringing behavioural changes in children of 8 to 10 years of age. He observed a significant change in the mood of these children from irritating to normal after administration of music to them.

Dr. Bhattacharya (1970) of the M.S. University, Baroda, used various *Ragas* like the *Bihag, Lalit* and *Jaijaiwanti* for the cure of mentally retarded and mentally ill, institutionalized 50 persons who were aggressive, depressed, worried, slow-learners etc. and found that these *Ragas* had beneficial effect on the experimental subjects.

Thakur (1981) reported that the effect of *Raga Bhairavi* as observed by Pandit Ravi Shankar is quite extensive since it aroused the emotions of the listener. Similar effect of the other *Ragas* like the *Adana, Darbari-Kanhara, Khamaj, Purvi, Basant, Sorath, Hindole, Marwa, Puriya, Tilang, Bilawal, Ramkali, Kalingra, Sohni, Kamod, Paraj, Multani, Todi, Bhairav, Malkauns, Piloo, Bahar, Rageshawari, Dhani, Bihag* and others was also observed.

Folk Songs and Popular Songs

These songs are based on the social life of the society in which a particular sect or community of individuals are living and are, thus, confined to local areas only. These are being passed on from generation to generation and as such are neither old nor new. They are associated with the life of common people, composed in simple tunes and popular and simple language so that every individual can understand and sing them with ease and without technical knowledge of music. These songs do not need any sophisticated musical instrument for accompaniment during their singing. Whatever the musical instruments are needed, they are made locally with the local materials. Such songs are usually sung in groups where the performers are themselves the participants. All this makes such songs very popular with the listeners and participants and may leave a long lasting effect on the feelings and emotions of individuals.

Folk Music and Popular Music

Folk music is an integral part of the social and cultural life of a society. Its effect on the mind and behaviour of the individual expressed as arousal of emotions and feelings, has been studied by a number of musicologist in many countries.

This has been described as "Typically folk music lives in oral tradition: it is learnt through learning rather than reading. It is functional in the sense that it is associated with other activities. Folk music is understood by broad segments of the population and is disseminated within families and restricted social networks. Above all, perhaps the most important characteristic of a folk song is its dependence on acceptance by a community, that is, by a village, nation, or family, and its tendency to change as is passed down from one individual to another". (International Folk Music Council Yearbook, 1969).

Shanti Goverdhan (1957) had described the folk songs as an indicator of the political, social, religious, economic, historical and cultural activities of the area from which they had originated. As such the listener becomes highly involved in it and may start to dance with the tune because it affects the feelings and behaviour of the listener.

Teodor Bratu (1970), a Romanian music composer drew attention to the use of local folk-lore in these songs, stressing that national identity in music for children was important educationally as it acquainted them with the national artistic values handed down the generations: developed the feelings of gratitude and devotion to their country and the working people — the makers of all the material and spiritual values : and helped to raise them in the spirit of humaneness, in a spirit of friendship and respect for all nationals in the world.

Kaufmann (1979) observed that participation in the recreation of traditional folk songs increased the acquisition of native language among them and because of simplicity, folk songs are suitable for young children.

General Achievements

Improvement in the general achievements of young people has often been reported by various music educators. Children studying in general education schools with music tutions experience a richer world of moods and feelings. Their musical studies help them to do better in other subjects, not only because of specific ties between those subjects but because music also builds up the overall tone, increases the pupils joy of living and desire to work (Mihalyi, 1970).

In the words of Erzsebet Szonyi quoted by Sarai (1970) from an article in 'Tempo' — "daily music lessons very quickly develop in small children a sense of rhythm, and technique of clear singing expressiveness and interpretation and they train the memory and encourage accuracy. Listening to listen to tempo and dynamics has a favourable effect on the child's sensibility and develops feasibility to express his feelings, thanks to which the child's imagination is enriched and the feelings he writes and paints are the richer too... Thanks to often singing together with others, he acquires a better developed sense of group awareness than those who have not had the good fortune to have such lessons."

Listening to and Participation in Music

Music listening is a wonderful experience. It is an art which involves both the performer and the listener. Both of them are important as far as the psychological effect is concerned. Schopenhauer (1883) acknowledged a connection between human feelings and music : which, "restores to us all the emotions of our inmost nature, but entirely without reality and far removed from their pain. Music when presented as an analogue of the emotional life, is a copy or symbol of the will."

According to Copland (1952), Sidney Licht, a fellow of New York Academy of Medicines, who contributed a great deal to the results of research into music therapy, wrote, "I am convinced that listeners are physiologically and psychologically affected by such musical characteristics as mood, intensity, pitch, and rhythmically outline and this should provoke rememberance and association of thoughts more easily in a mental patient than methods using factual persuation."

Copland (1952) observed that listening to music is an emotional experience or an intellectual exercise which depends upon receptivity and knowledge in music of the listener. Deva (1967) found that a person lacking technical knowledge of music may feel it as emotions an experienced listener may speak to himself or view the experience as in the strictly descriptive musical terms.

Klitz (1970) suggested that music participation helps to increase the power of concentration and attention span thus, facilitating relaxation, encouraging better posture and proper breathing, improving coordination, strengthening specific muscle groups, removing frustrations and reducing emotional tensions.

Deva (1970) correlated the effect of Indian music on the Indian listener and provided a schematic outline starting from encoder (musician) performing *Raga* with the emotion and motivation through the frequency, intensity, complexity and modulation of *Raga* and *Tala* etc. to the decoder (listener) whose auditory perception, emotions and social conditions were observed.

Przychodzinska-Kaciczak (1970), a scientist of Poland working in music reported that —i) emotional experience derived from music has an influence on the formation of one's moral and intellectual outlook, ii) music activities develop imagination and creative thinking when confronted with such challenges as to create simple music, etc. and iii) contact with music has an influence on the cognitive process, that is, it has the help of music on the development of child's thinking, its role as a source of

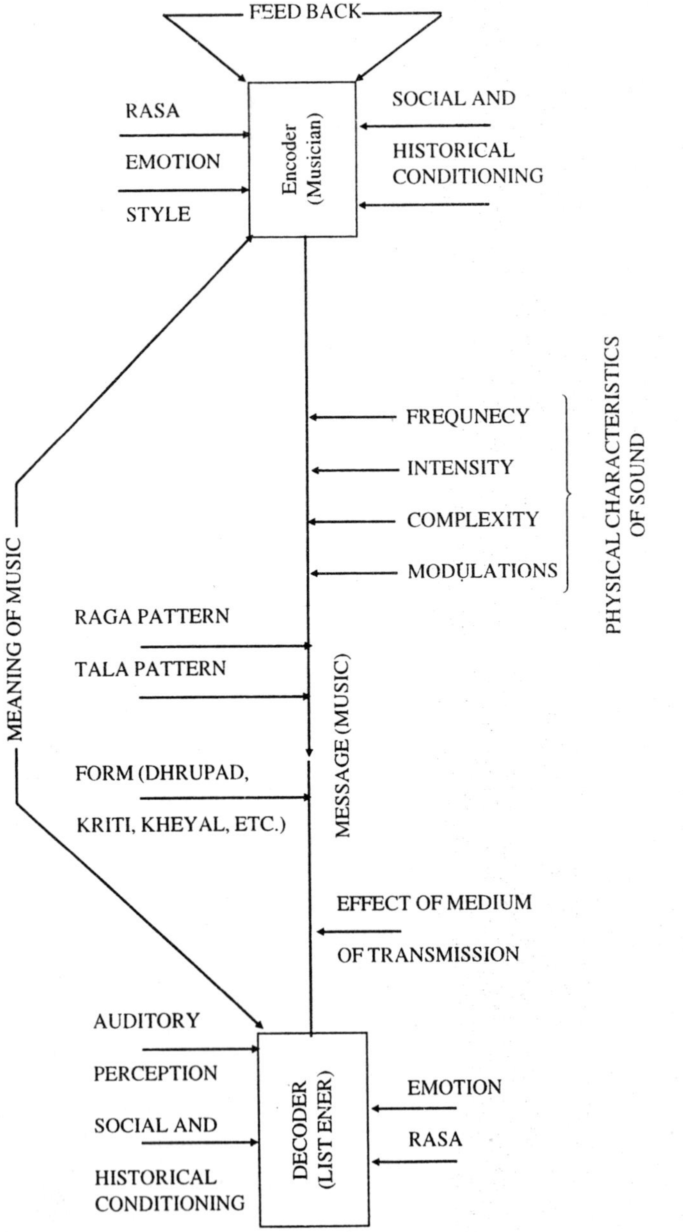

Fig. *Music as a communicative process (Adapted from Deva 1970)*

knowledge and deeper understanding of the world, and finally, the significance of music as an element in mustering humanism.

Kaufmann (1979) found that active participation in the recreation of folk songs by the young children, counteracted the deleterious effect of passivity in the participants.

Educating the Mentally Handicapped Children

Among the different categories of mentally handicapped children, the mild and the moderate mentally retarded children may be brought to the level of average children with the help of special education designed for them.

Effect of music has been studied on average students and it has been acclaimed as an important tool for bringing the significant improvement in the academic field and other behaviours. Cyril Burt (1969) has suggested that the capacities of mentally handicapped children in musical ability, are as good as those of average children of the same age. Further, music education has been employed as a means of improving the academic achievement and social adjustment of mentally handicapped children so that they feel themselves as a part of the society.

Various research workers (Leslie, 1981 and Frank, 1981) have reported significant improvement in academic achievement and adjustment in school, of mentally handicapped children as a result of education.

Music education provided to these handicapped children may bring significant improvement in their school adjustment and achievement so as to bring them at par with the average student of the same age. Very little attention is being paid to the improvement of mentally handicapped children in India. Facilities exist only for 0.2 per cent of such children for their development in the schools and other institutions (Desai, 1981).

Chapter 3

PERSPECTIVES OF MUSIC EDUCATION

THE arts — poetry, music and architecture, painting and sculpture arouse an intense feeling and urge to experience and appreciate both the sensible and the super-sensible objects and though at first their representatives are indirect in terms of the physical expressions, yet they directly appeal to the depth of experience or feeling, and create aesthetic joy and beauty. Music is absolutely concerned with the problems of emotional content, value and beauty. The philosophy of music like many other branches of knowledge, claims attention on intellectual grounds than on utilitarian grounds.

Musical experience contains the enquiries into various musical problems like, 1) the musical sounds, 2) the nature of the simplest elementary modes in which the material is arranged or prepared for use, 3) the distinction between two varieties of music, known as melody and harmony, alongwith other musical materials like counter point, time, measure, rhythm and form of music. And broadly speaking, says Dr. Pole "We may fairly assume that the principles which have determined or influenced them, may be classed under two heads, namely, physical principles and aesthetical principles. By physical principles we mean such principles as can be deduced, according to the laws of natural sciences, from the physical nature of musical sounds and from their known physiological effects on the human ear. Aesthetical principles, are such principles as have resulted from the free action of the human mind, independently of any physical consideration.

The main material of music consists of tones and sounds, and philosophical concept of music, centres around this sound theory.

India is known as the country of spirituality. Here philosophy of music is regarded as a spiritual *Sadhana* which elevates the level of man's consciousness and kindles in the cave of his heart, the perceptual light of divine knowledge and makes him free from the den of delusion forever and ever. the intuitive anchors of music of India, are fully conscious of this secret, and have made music the best and purest means for attaining the realization of God. The philosophical foundation of music rests upon the solid rock of the realization of the immortal soul of music. Therefore, we should be educated to know the soul of music, because proper training and education can only harmonize the choice of phenominal music with those of the transcendential grand music of man. The artists as well as the art of music should, therefore, be raised upon the high level of spirituality and they should be conscious of the ground truth of philosophy *(Darshanshastra)* of India; that man can see God face to face, can get an immediate awareness of the Absolute, as the task of philosophy of India is to solve the riddle of the universe and to discover the ways and means to man's perfection in life.

Psychological aspect of music is exclusively concerned with the awakening of the flashes of the primal psychic force-centre. The study in the psychology of music brings into us a clear understanding as well as an intutive perception of utility and importance of the force-centre, and it gives us a full realisation and the real objects and ideal of the musical contents. The great laboratories like those of Bell Telephones Company, and Harward and

Iowa Universities of America, have made considerable researches on psychological aspects of music, which have enriched the Western musicology.

People sing and dance to express their feelings of joy and sorrow. They enjoy, lament and express their awe and reverence through the medium of colourful tones and balanced rhythms of songs and dances. It is because the psychic centre that lies within him, stirs his emotions and makes him to create, project and enjoy music. It may be called the emotional side of the musical experience, which is known as sensuous appreciation and creation or projection. But psychologists, Revesz of Holland and Seashore of America are of the opinion that though the concept of musicality is attached to the psychology of music, yet the musical experience in relation to emotion and sensuous appreciation are not entire thing in the field of musicality.

The aesthetic content is an important thing in the domains of psychology and philosophy of music, and it should be experienced and appraised. But such an experience is mental or psychological in its characters, and so it must be inwardly digested and fashioned. It must be taken to note that a musical person having musical taste is possessed by a deep understanding of musical form and structure together with the inward tendency of the musical person to dive deep into the mood of music and get a relation to it which has an effect on his whole spiritual being.

Psychologically, music education influences the all-round development of the child. This influence manifests itself in three ways :

1. Music promotes development of in the sphere of the emotions alongwith developing the child's cognitive abilities. The emotional experience

derived from music has an influence on the formation of child's normal and intellectual outlook.

2. Music activities tend to develop imagination and creative thinking. A child when confronted with such challenges, as having to create simple music, he puts his mind to work, tries to cope with the tasks of his own, becomes accustomed to independent artistic expression, and gains confidence in his own creative powers. Unquestionably, all this is carried over to other spheres of thought and activity.

3. Contact with music has an influence on the cognitive processes. The significance of music on child's thinking and its role as a source of knowledge and deep understanding of the world acts as an element in nurturing humanism and the child developes a penetrating way of cognizing the surrounding world with the help of music.

Exceptional Children

These are the children who deviate socially, mentally or physically from the average children to such an extent that they require major modifications of the usual school practices in order to develop to their full capacities. Mentally retarded children who are usually intellectually limited or subnormal, appear to be substantially below the average child in learning ability and find it difficult to cope with the programme of regular grade levels.

Research on the personal adjustment of handicapped children has shown the possibility of maladjustment to be as great as common sense would indicate. Personal adjustment of the mentally handicapped is contingent upon many factors, among which the most important is excessive frustration of the child in his growing years when there is a discrepency between his ability to perform and the requirements of the environment. During the pre-school years, the mentally handicapped child is a major concern of his parents whose anxiety leads them to seek diagnosis and cures from many sources.

In his early school years, the mentally handicapped child meets more obstacles to development when in competition with the average child. Studies have shown that when the mentally retardates are assigned to regular grade without special provisions made for them, they tend to be isolated because they are usually rejected by their normal class-mates.

Since their experience in the school tends to be that of failure, mentally retarded pupils are in danger of developing emotional maladjustment. The school programme too are geared upon the average pupil. The bright pupils are able to slide along but the retarded children are forced to face failure and thus, experience feelings of frustration. In a school situation of this kind, the mentally retarded child learns to feel that he is and will be a failure in life, his ambition is ignored, stunted or destroyed and he is led to believe that he can never succeed.

The adolescent age is difficult for mentally retarded children, as is for all other children. At this age level, more personal and social problems appear and to combat with these problems , special provisions are not made available in the schools. Many mentally handicapped children are unable to cope with the more abstract and academic requirements of the schools at this age level, hence there is a great need for special education programme.

Education of Mentally Retarded

In order to lessen their dependence on society and to develop their capablities, mentally retarded children are often provided with programme of special education.

Special education involves adaptation of the curriculum, the teaching techniques or the organizational programme. It refers to only those aspects of education that are unique or are added to the regular programmes of the school. The amount and kind of adaptation needed depends upon many factors including the type of deviation and the degree of deviation.

Mental handicap affects 2 to 3 per cent of most populations all over the world, and severe degrees (Intelligence Quotient under 50) of it affects 4 per 1000 general population. Exact figures for India are not available, though a few prevalence surveys have been done yielding widely desperate figures. If we calculate the prevalence of mental handicap in India according to the usual world prevalence, we get the enormous figure of 12 to 18 million affected persons and 2.4 million severely retardates in the total population. With India's growth rate of 2.2 per cent per year, an annual incidence of 0.3 to 0.4 million mentally handicapped persons can be expected in our population every year — many of them being due to preventable causes. Apart from humane consideration, this is a tremendous waste of life and of scarce resources.

Services for the handicapped are so meagre that they do not even cover one per cent of the mentally handicapped. In other words, over 99 per cent of the mentally handicapped in India have to do without care of any type, beyond what can be provided for them by their own families. Medical diagnostic and therapeutic facilities are only available in the larger cities. Most doctors are not interested in mental handicap, as they think nothing much can be done about it—a totally wrong concept. An equally highly unsatisfactory state of services for the handicapped exists in all other fields — educational, vocational, residential, employment, legislation, insurance etc. Services are practi-cally non-existent as compared to the need.

In the educational field, there are facilities catering to a maximum of 10,000 children, approximately 0.04 per cent of the number of the mentally handicapped in India, estimating prevalence at only the 4 per 1000 figures given for severe mental handicap. These centres are all concentrated in a few towns, leaving most of the country bereft of all facilities. These institutions are, by and large, poorly staffed and inadequately equipped. Very few teachers have some training in special education or techniques of educating the mentally handicapped. Teaching equipment is highly inadequate in many, and almost completely lacking in some so called institutes for the mentally handicapped.

Legislation for the mentally handicapped in India is prehistoric, being governed by the Indian Lunacy Act of 1912 which equates the mentally handicapped with the psychiatrically abnormal, depriving them of their fundamental rights. As far as social security is concerned, their is no such thing for the mentally handicapped.

Community awareness about mental handicap is also very deficient. Most of the public consider the mentally handicapped as insane. Complete ignorance about the condition, its causes and the fact that they are capable of development and productivity, is the general rule. Even many educated persons consider it a waste of money and resources to do anything for the mentally handicapped. They forget that for very little input, a great deal of mental handicap could be completely prevented.

Declaration by the United Nations on the right of mentally retarded persons brought into sharp focus for the general public, the fact that such persons remained under-priveledged, deprived of their full rights and were unable to develop their potentials. The work carried out in professional circles revealed that great majority of this group are mildly mentally retardates and that when they receive appropriate education, have scope to become independent and live as members of the society. The principle of normalization gained wide acceptance and became an important guiding principle in providing community care. The diverse nature of the condition, as highlighted by research work, called for the close co-ordination of different disciplines. Embodied in one of the basic promises of the W.H.O. (1968), is this basic truth that "no single discipline has the knowledge or the competence to undertake alone the responsibility of meeting the needs of the mentally retarded."

The education of mentally defective children is a question on which opinions are divided. There is no doubt that this kind of teaching is generally organised in countries where education is most advanced, for there it has been realized that it is equally useful for children and teachers in ordinary classes to be relieved of a dead weight, and for backward pupils, who are definitely imprevious to ordinary teaching, to be dealt with by themselves. On this point, there is general agreement that the existence of classes for mentally defective alongwith normal children is generally a mark of well organised for educational system.

It sometimes happens, however, even in countries where this special teaching has been most eagerly undertaken, that when the first wave of enthusiasm has passed, people begin to wonder how far it is wise, from the social standpoint to devote so much money and effort-including in many cases the flower of the teaching profession children who will never pull more than half their weight in society, no matter what you do for them. And there is obviously a certain amount of truth in this point of view.

But there is another way of visualising this question. Is it not the duty of the society, on social and humanitarian grounds, to do as much as possible for these poor creatures of whom many, though not all, are the victims of defects in our existing social system. In the great industrial centres, where economic conditions are most unfavourable, the proportion of defective children increases most rapidly. Is it not also our duty to replace the ordinary school, which to these poor children is a place of torment, by a school more suited to their tastes and aptitudes, and thus to provide them with a little of the happiness of which they will be largely deprived when their school days are over.

Mental retardation has for long been considered as being a condition with no clear cut generalized anatomical, bio-chemical or physiological abnormalities, as being a condition equally susceptible to the vagaries of social and environmental factors. In the latter context, conditions of rapid technological development and social change, merely augument existing problems of the mentally retarded population. In countries which are in the midst of such transitional phase like the Indian society, that the steps be taken, with deeper insight for the elimination of human misery and amelioration of the lot of mentally retarded children.

It is particularly from the pedagogical stand-point however, that we find the most ample justification for the sacrifices that we make in the interests of defective childhood. For the result of thus, adopting the school to the needs of the feeble-minded has been the evolution of methods and procedures which has proved just as excellent in the education of normal children.

Aims of Special Education

In advance countries, special education of mentally retarded children has become relatively universal. It aims at training the mentally retardates — (1) academically, to the level of an average child, (2) socially, in adjustment to the home and community, and (3) occupationlly, in being able to support themselves totally or partially at the adult level.

Experts recommended a special type of education to help the retardates to develop skills necessary to live as happily and socially competent as an average child and later as an adult. Special education recommended aims at helping the mentally retardates to raise their level of functioning. Experts have also found that quite a remarkable development is possible with their early detection and early introduction of special education course. The determination of the child's eligibility for social programmes is made by psychologists. In making their assessment, psychologists take into account other criteria such as school adjustment and an evaluation of the adjustment of the child in the regular grades.

The goals of special education for mentally retarded children are similar to the goals of education for ordinary children, but only the techniques for attaining them are different.

One of the most important aspects of the education of the mentally handicapped is attitudinal — that is, preparing the child for adapting to the world outside the classroom and facing his handicap in such a way as to permit him to lead a relatively normal life. The mentally retardates obviously require prolonged periods of intensive and individualized instructions which include special techni-ques to maintain, interest more active participation and much repetition of similar material in various forms.

The special education programmes for mentally retardates aims to attain the following purposes :

1. To help severely withdrawn mentally retardates to take interest in themselves and their surroundings through simple, non-threatening manipulation activities.
2. To encourage re-socialisation.
3. To provide outlet for impulses of aggression and hostility.
4. To yield pleasure rather than failure in accomplishment and in the growth of personal skills.
5. To provide and reinforce important social traits such as cooperation, group awareness, sensitivity etc. to others and a realistic view of one's own social behaviour.
6. To establish patterns of recreational involvement and interests that will carry over to life in the community.
7. Above all, the major goal of special education (beyond developing skills and imparting information), is the ultimate adjustment of the mentally handicapped to the society of average individuals.

Such special education programmes, whether their purpose be to improve vocational competence, develop potential abilities or simply improve the quality of living for a group that too often has been condemned to a barren and hopeless kind of existence, provide a challenge that cannot be ignored by thoughtful citizens.

Music Education as A Special Education Programme

Second only to physical education in terms of its potential for special education, is the school music programme. Music and the arts were frequently employed as therapeutical agents in ancient societies. Today, it is felt and believed that arts may be used for clinical purposes and to assist in the development of desired psychological or physical behaviour. With the application of experimental approach to the use of music, E.Thayer Gasten (1968) defined three functions of music as a means of special education :

1. Establishment or re-establishment of inter-personal relationships.
2. Bringing about of self-esteem through self-actualization.
3. Utilization of the unique potential of rhythm to energise and to bring order.

Music study and its performance have been recognized as subject areas ever since Lowell Mason, the first music teacher in American Public Schools, began teaching music in the Howes School in Boston in 1838. Despite this long history, the use of music education as the special education programme for handicapped has not made its place as an integral part of educational programme designed for them.

Musical performance can be among the most satisfying parts of group activities. It allows individuals the opportunity for self-expression through the subordination of personal interest for the benefit of group. This form of self-expression is socially acceptable and tends to support the development of cooperation within the peer group. The individual has the opportunity to become aware of his identity and his accomplishment by comparing these with those of the group. With expansion of the size of the group, the subject learns to relate with flexibility to a variety of social units and develops a capacity to relate to a variety of social institutions. In combination with regular classroom activities, music education provides a non-threatening experiences which assist individuals and groups to self-realization by means of process that is expressive and socially rewarding.

The Need

A child, whether average or the mentally retarded must be brought up in a congenial environment with all the material and conditions that serve to stimulate his moral functions. A child wants to be recognised for his creativity and personal status. For gaining self-confidence, interest, initiative, instinctive needs for activity and achievement, he does his utmost attempts. It is the music which provides keen delight, encouragement, inspiration and modifies the emotions, thus, it points out the very fact that music is the sole agent of therapeutic use for the development of mentally retarded children.

Music therapy offers new hope for the mentally retarded and handicapped children, spastics, neurotics, insomanioc, depressed, aged, blind, drug addicts are also among those who could benefit by this therapy.

In Western countries, music therapy has become a systematic discipline with a clear cut methodology but in India, however, there is a dearth of scientifically collected data on the therapeutic use of music.

Experts in this field say that the truth in music therapy is neither in the exaggerated claims by musicians and persons connected with alternative systems of medicine nor in the casual way in which professors in medicine and psychiatrists dismiss the therapeutic benefits of music. The effect can be known by a judicious blend of science and arts with therapy for a select group of patients.

It needs skill, patience and training of the teachers to bring about the desired effects. The therapeutic programme of music must be done with the team work of specially trained teacher, musicians, psychologists and physicians to acheive the maximum success.

Chapter 4

MENTAL RETARDATION

MENTAL Retardation is a condition in which the individual's intelligence is less than that of the average individual : there are few things he can do and some he can not do and as such he is not useless. But he will do these things more slowly than an individual of normal intelligence, he may be able to perform as a normal person at a later age.

Mental retardation or mental handicap as it is now termed, is defined as significantly sub-average general intellectual functioning, — existing concurrently with defecits in adaptive behaviour, and manifested during the developmental period. The developmental period is taken as up to the age of 18 years. Adaptive behaviour is defined as the effectiveness with which an individual meets the standards of personal independence and social responsibility expected of his age and cultural group.

Definition

Various psychologists and investigators have put forward many definitions. Some of the most common and accepted are as follows :

Kirk (1970) has defined the exceptional child as 'that child who deviates from the average or normal child in mental, physical and social characteristics to such an extent that he requires modification of school practices or special educational services in order to develop his maximum capacity'! This definition is a broad-based one which may be applied to both the categories of exceptional children that is, the gifted and the mentally handicapped. Therefore, he gave another definition of the mentally handicapped child as "the one having sub-average intelligence and intellectual functioning and hence finds it difficult to cope with the performance of regular grade levels."

The definition adopted by the American Society of Mental Deficiency (Herber 1961) refers mental retardation to sub-average general intellectual functioning which originate during the developmental period and is associated with impairment in adaptive behaviour.

According to British Joint Committee on Mental Deficiency, the term Mental Retarded Child is used in broader sense to include all those whose educational progress, from whatever cause, has been slower than that of an average child of the same chronological age. (The New Encyclopaedia Britannica, Vol.IX, 1973-74).

The terms which are used interchangeably with mental retardation are mentally backward, mentally handicapped, mental deficiency, feablemindedness, oligophrenia, amentia and sub-normal mental development.

In general, the mental retarded children are sub-normal in assuming their responsibilities which are expected from socially adequate children, such as self-direction, self-support and social participation. These children usually have low degree of intellectual development.

Characteristics

The effects of impaired levels of intellectual and social functioning are maximally manifested in the dimension of personality of the individual. No person is born with unadaptive patterns of reacting and nor is the personality (at birth) warped. The clean state of mind, is fashioned by the experiences which follow. The mentally retarded child, confronted with repeated failures and non-acceptance by others reacts accordingly—as an intellectually normal child would, given the circumstances. This understanding has been generated by the wealth of research literature available. Some studies conducted in India have revealed that mentally retarded children are more extrovert and less neurotic than their normal counterparts. This extroversion is exhibited in the greater amounts of persistence evidence. Studies on the quality of adjustment of the adolescent mentally retarded boys have shown that the degree of maladjustment is significantly more in the home, health, social and emotional spheres than the normal ones in normal intelligence, since maladjustment is rational precursor of maldaptive behaviour. The results of two separate studies came as no surprise. Singh and Dagar (1982), in an attempt to determine the socio-economic co-relates of scholastic achievements, speech and conduct disorders, delinquent and neurotic/psychotic behaviours observed that the family structure, parents education, economic level and employment of mother significantly influence the behaviour among mentally retarded children. Chawla and Neki (1978) found from a clinical survey that the female mental retardates had behaviour problems such as aggressive reactions.

Mentally retarded child is often hyperactive i.e. he rushes about from one thing to another, being constantly on move. He cannot attend to one thing for more than a few minutes at a time since his concentration is poor, his memory span is short, laughs at one moment and cries the next, good in some subjects and may be poor at others, especially. Arithmetic and shows quick change in behaviour. These children are often very anxious though their parents may not know it. Anxiety makes them ritualistics. They cling to familiar objects and routines and want to do everything in exactly the same way every day, and get very angry and upset if there is slight change in the environment.

Mental retardation involves marked difficulties in cognition and personality development while it is true that no two mentally retarded individuals like their normal counterparts, learn or develop in the same way. It is also true that all mentally retarded children experience severe difficulties in the development of skills necessary to live as members of the community. This reveals a fundamental challenge. The fundamental difference between normal and mentally retarded children lies in their (mentally retarded) inability to learn by observation and imitation in the low levels of natural curiousity necessary for experimentation and exploration.

The group of sub-average general intellectual functioning individuals includes all whose performance on suitable objective tests of general intellectual ability is more than one standard deviation below the population mean. The upper limit of the developmental period is considered to be at approximately eighteen years.

Adaptive behaviour is manifested in three principal manners, 1) Maturation, 2) Learning and, 3) Social adjustment. Each of these three factors assume primary importance during a certain stage of the developmental period. Thus, maturation, which refers to the rate of development of sensory motor skills such as sitting, walking, talking, is the important criterion of adaptive behaviour during the pre-school years. Learning defined as ability to acquire academic skill, is important during the school age years. Social adjustment assumes primary importance at the adult level. The principal indicators of social adjustment at the adult level are : "the degree to which the individual is able to maintain himself independently in the community and in gainful employment as well as by his ability to meet and to conform to other personal and social responsibilities and standards set by the community" (Herber, 1959).

The quality of interpersonal relationship is an important manifestation of adaptive behaviour during the pre-school and school periods. However, social adjustment is considered as the primary criterion of adaptive behaviour only at the adult level.

Studies of mentally retarded children's social adjustment have varied with regard to the definition and measures of social adjustment . None have employed the term in a strictly clinical sense which incorporates in-depth interview of children's feelings. Most investigations have relied on perceptions of others, or the mentally retarded child's own perception of his social functioning. A few investigators have employed direct observations of E M R (educable mentally retarded) children in the classroom in an effort to study their social adjustment.

While peer ratings have usually revealed that integrated E M R are not more highly accepted by their classmates than segregated children. E M R pupil's self reports have indicated that integrated children have a more positive attitude towards school and a better self concept than segregated pupils. The realm of knowledge in the field of mental retardation has expanded over the last twenty years. Certain kinds of mental retardation can be prevented or even treated if detected early enough. In the sphere of education, the mentally retarded is capable of far more learning than thought possible before, if when, proper training and adequate facilities are provided. Any improvement now made can only accrue from the drive towards 'better care and understanding' than from mere technologies.

Mentally retarded children are not born difficult to cure or treat but they become so because of the way they have been treated. Because of their low intelligence they cannot do as well as their normal brothers and sisters. If the parents show their disappointment, the child reacts by anxiety and later, either withdraws or refuses to do anything, even those things which he can do. Further, the child may show hostility, aggression, temper tantrums and antisocial behaviour.

These children feel themselves as neglected part of the society and may suffer from many complexes : lack of self-control, poor judgement of self-understanding, inferiority complex, frustration etc., therefore, they usually display impulsive behaviour, emotional instability, excitability, depression and apathy . Apart from this, they are slow learners and have low degree of intelligence as compared to average children. Such children, due to having low intelligence, are not able to cope with the performance of regular grade level and so remain as such or lag behind the average student in academic achievement and adjustment in the school and at home.

Causes

Even four thousand years ago when the Ayurveda, the book on Indian medicines was conceptualized, mental retardation was not left out. *Charaka* — the father of Indian medicines and the *Sushruta* — the father of Indian surgery, hypothesized that mental retardation or *Manasmandyain* was result of defective genes, poor conditions during pregnancy and faulty child rearing practices, in the same manner as it is understood even today. *Charaka's* explanation of the role played by the parental seed or the germ-plasm in subsequently personality development incorporates concepts now recognized as Darwin's gemmule' and Spencer's 'Concepts'. However, both the Charak Samhita and the *Sushruta Samhita* professed reservations about the genetic basis of mental retardation, instead they emphasized the influence of divine forces and the *Grahas* (astronomical stars) to be the cause of mental retardation. This thinking, in which the present, past and future are attributed to supernatural power, typifies Indian philosophical thought with its belief in the *Karma*, accepted in large part even today.

Our understanding of mental retardation has certainly come a long way since the time of Charak and Sushruta. Mental retardation is not a single disease with a single cause. It has multiple causes and can manifest as a symptom of many different types of diseases and syndroms. These causes may be genetic or environmental and may include pre-natal as well as post-natal causes. Mental retardation may be due to variety of reasons, such as genetic or chromosomic accident, under development birth trauma, viral diseases affecting the central nervous system or brain damage. It is not curable when it is associated with physical disability and epilepsy. Among the common illness encountered by the parent are the common cold, asthma and sore throat which involve the respiratory system; while diarrhoea and dysentry (stool containing mucus and blood) involving gastrointestinal tract. Problems associated with the central nervous system are generally localized to the sense organs in its mild form and the brain with more serious effects (as in maningitis and encephalitis). The diseases which can afflict a child are many, ranging from the mild to the most severe and involving major systems of the body.

The chances of genetically determined mental handicap increase when blood relatives marry: higher in such children than in the children of parents who are not blood relatives. It has been established that nearer the blood relation, the higher are the chances of mental handicap. Mental retardation is caused by many genetic factors. Chromosomal causes or disorders are the main genetic factors responsible for mental retardation. An upset of this genetic balance results in an upset of metabolism of the cells. Children with severe mental retardation or with Darwin's syndrome are retarded in physical and mental growth which is undoubtedly related to the presence of the extra chromosomal gene inheritance pattern or certain well established hereditary diseases that cause mental retardation. Most authorities agree that certain types of mental retardation have genetic origin but the environmental causes also affect the mental growth. The problem revolves around the interaction of heredity and environment. Intelligence undoubtedly is the result of multiple gene inheritance interacting with environment.

Identification

In order to identify the mentally handicap, Indian studies followed the Western model till as late as the 1930, with the movement towards 'Indianisation' of research, which gained momentum only in the sixties. Though psychological principles remain culture-free, their interpretation can only retain impetus when the mileu is considered. The direction of the movement was as first, more towards the adaptation of intelligence tests, and the establishment of norm, than towards reconstruction of such tests. The movement began with the efforts of Rice in 1929, with the adaptation of the Binet Scales. Twenty years later, Kamath adopting a more scientific approach, revised the earlier adaptation and translated it into several regional languages. It has only been since the last two decades that Indian researchers have completely accepted the movement. Later on, most popular tests of intelligence, behaviour, and personality were adapted and translated into regional languages, thus paving the way for identifying mentally handicapped population with more precise and scientific approach.

Intelligence Quotient

Intelligence Quotient (IQ) is a rough measure of child's intelligence compared to that of an average child. It is measured by giving the child specific tests. The IQ measurement is not infallible, there can be many mistakes in its measurement due to the following factors:

(1) A child who is not familiar with the kind of situations used in testing will score lower than his actual intelligence.

(2) The same will happen if a child is sick, tired, sleepy, afraid of the examiner or uninterested in the test.

Therefore, a number of repeat tests must be done before the IQ can be said to actually indicate a child's intelligence. Different scores given by different examiners can be explained by discrepancies arising form the above two points.

Both, the degree of intellectual impairment, and of social incompetence of the individual in relation to his environment should be considered in determining this. Intellect is comprised of many processes : perception, memory, recognition, conceptualization, convergent and divergent reasoning (classification and creativity), verbal facility and motor competence. Intelligence tests have been devised to measure different parameters of intelligence in the different age groups. The Intelligence Quotient (IQ) is calculated by chronological age multiplied by 100.

The assessment of IQ is satisfactory because it is one of the measures for determination of the extent to which a child is able to master academic school requirement. Although data concerning the child's physical condition, his emotional stability, and his home conditions will also be needed for identification of mental retardation, yet the I Q will be an important factor in making this decision.

Levels of Measured Intelligence

Various investigations have been carried out to find as to how the intelligence is distributed in the population as a whole. As a sample of the complete range of the I Q which may be expected in an unselected school population, the standardization sample for the Stanford-Binet Scale is perhaps the most representative. On this scale, the distribution of the I Qs of 2904 children, ranging in age from 2 to 18 years is shown in the following table.

Table showing the I Q range$

I Q	No.	Percentage	Classification
160-169	1	0.03	Very superior
150-159	6	0.02	
140-149	32	1.1	
130-139	89	3.1	Superior
120-129	239	8.2	
110-119	524	18.1	Bright
100-109	685	23.5	Average
90-99	667	23.0	
80-89	422	14.5	Below average
70-79	164	5.6	Slow, borderline defective
60-69	57	2.0	Mentally retarded defective
50-59	12	0.4	
40-49	6	0.2	Mentally retarded
30-39	1	0.03	

$ Adapted from M.A.Merrill

Children rated upon the Stanford Revision of the Binet-Simon Test approximate a normal distribution if the group is non-selected and if there are enough cases. Terman (1916) measured the I Q of 1, 000 'representative children'. The distribution is shown in figure given below. The variation from 100 for equal percentages to the right and the left are not identical, but they are nearly so. The distribution is approximately normal.

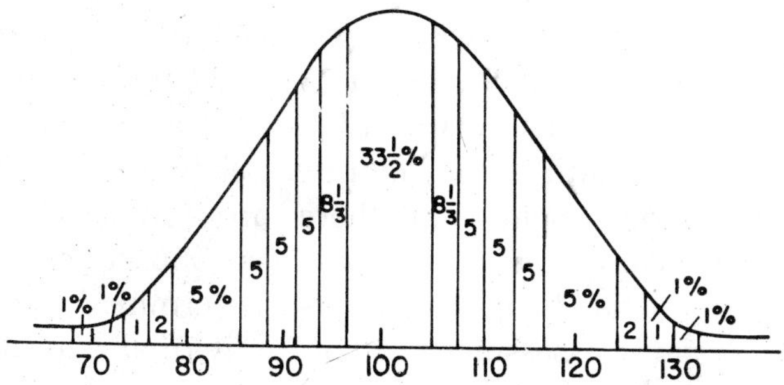

Percentage Distribution of I Qs of 1000 Children

This figure shows how children vary continuously from a very low IQ to a very high I, Q. The percentages above and below the given I Q levels vary slightly in this figure from percentages more recently discovered, but the figure still represents well the concept of a normal distribution. For the purpose of forming special classes, an I Q under 70 is very commonly used. According to recent testing based upon Terman's 1936 revision of the Binet-Simon Test, 3 per cent of the population is under the I Q 70.

The classification of adaptive behaviour is more complex than measured intelligence because of the former's lack of objective measures. The level of retardation in adaptive behaviour is also expressed in standard deviation units accompanied by descriptions.

The Vineland Social Maturity Scale — supplemented where necessary for portions of the Gestalt Developmental Schedules, the Cattell Infant Intelligence Scale, and the Kuhlmann Test of Mental Development — is recommended for use at the pre-school level as a measure of adaptive behaviour. During the school age period, standardized achievement tests will be the primary measure, though the Vineland Test still will be used to differentiate between the lower levels of retardation. At the adolescent and adult level, adaptive behaviour is best seen in social adjustment, but there are few instruments available that assess this behaviour. Subsequently, the level of social adjustment is determined by the diagnostician's assessment of the individual's social and vocational adjustment.

The following table summarizes the levels of measured intelligence.

Table showing levels of measured intelligence

Word description of retardation in measured Intelligence	Level of deviation in measured intelligence	Range in Standard deviation Value	Corresponding IQ range for test	
			Stanford-Binet	Wechler
			SD - 16	SD - 15
Borderline	-1	-1.01 to-2.0	68-83	70-84
Mild	-2	-2.01 to--3.0	52-67	55-69
Moderate	-3	-3.01 to-4.0	36-51	40-54
Severe	-4	-4.01 to-5.0	20-35	25-39
Profound	-5	-5.0	Below 20	Below 25

Descriptions of the intellectual retardation are included under the corresponding IQ for the two most widely used 'individual intelligence tests': the 1960 revision of the Stanford Binet and the Weschsler Scales of Intelligence (Herber, 1961).

Types and Characteristics of Mentally Handicapped

The mentally handicapped or mentally retarded children are deficient in intelligence. They are also described as 'feeble minded' to denote all degrees of mental defect by arrested or defective mental development. They do not have enough intelligence to guide their own lives adequately, earn their own living with complete independence and make sensible judgements. The degree of mental deficiency varies and as such there are following categories of the mentally handicapped children.

1. Profound
2. Severe
3. Mederate
4. Mild
5. Border line

These categories are described as follows—

1. *Profound*

The IQ of this category of children is below 25. Most of the mental retardates in this category are severely deficient in adaptive behaviour and are unable to learn much even the simplest of tasks. Speech remains at a rudimentary level. Severe physical deformities, affected central nervous system and retarded growth are typical while convulsive seizures, mutism, deafness and other physical anomalies are common. These individuals require custodial care, so they may be either hospitalised or institutionalised. There general health and resistance to diseases is low and they may have a short life span.

2. *Severe*

These have also been termed as trainable mentally retardates (Kirk, 1970), their IQ ranges in between 50 and 25. They, because of sub-normal intelligence, are not capable of learning beyod, i) self-care, ii) adjustment to the home or neighbourhood, and iii) economic usefulness in the home. These children have severely retarded motor and speech development and have sensory defects. Such individuals can develop limited levels of personal hygiene and self-help skills, which in a way makes them less dependent but they require supervision and care throughout their lives.

3. *Moderate*

Children having the IQ range between 50 and 75 are termed as moderately deficient or educable mentally retarded children. Kirk (1970) has defined them as those who have potentials for development in, 1) minimum educability in the academic subjects of the school, 2) social adjustment to such a point that they can get along independently in the community, and 3) minimum occupational adequacy to such a degree that they can later support themselves partially or totally at the adult level. Intellectually these children are low in memory, language ability, imagination and creative abilities. Physically, these children usually appear clumsy and ungainly, and they suffer from bodily deformities and retarded motor co-ordination; they have frustration, intolerance, infantile play interests and are prone to delinquency. With early diagnosis, parental help and adequate opportunities for training, most of the moderate mental retardates can achieve partial independence in daily self-care, which is an acceptable behaviour in a family.

4. *Mild*

The children having the I Q range between 75 to 90 are called as mildly retarded children, some also term them as slow learners. The mental level of these children do not exceed the mental level of a normal child of 12 years. These children are unable to keep with the rest of the normal class in their rate of academic growth. Their motor skills and coordination are also somewhat inferior. Behaviourly, they are considered to be discipline problems, truants, inattentive and lazy. These children can be educated and can complete work upto the fifth primary class by the time they are sixteen. They are capable of benefitting by special training in reading, writing and arithmetic, and in some skilled and unskilled occupations. This group of mentally retarded but educable children constitute approximately 2.05 per cent of the population. At present they find their way into regular schools but find the usual school wok too difficult and are seldom able to make the grade.

5. *Border-Line*

This category comprises of the largest number of those labelled mentally retardates who are comparable to that of the average 8 to 11 years old child, since their I Q range is in between 55 and .69. Their social adjustment often approximates that of the adolescent, although they tend to lack the normal adolescents imagination, inventiveness and judgement. Ordinarily they do not show signs of brain imbalance or other physical anomalies. Often they require some measure of supervision due to their limited ability to foresee the consequences of their action. With timely diagnosis, parents assistance and special educational programmes, majority of them can adjust socially, master simple academic and occupational skills, and become self-supporting citizens.

Basic Needs Of Mentally Handicapped

Brian Klitz (1970) observed that the mentally retarded children have the same basic needs, urges and aspirations as that of the normal ones. The desire for social approval, personal recognition, prestige and accomplishment within their own framework of attainment remains strong and being given the exclusive attention of a teacher, may bring changes in their behaviour and academic achievements. According to Seeta Sinclair (1979) a retarded child's need are the same as those of a normally intelligent child. He requires lot of love and warmth, discipline which should be mild but consistent, and conditions in which he can develop his capabilities to the maximum. He needs a great deal of more patience and tolerance than a normal child.

Prevalence

The magnitude of the problem of mental retardation in a vast and populous country remains in the domain of estimations. There never has been a nation-wide survey, though several small scale studies have been carried out in several parts of our country. Despite the fact that techniques employed in each study have been different but, the findings provide some guidelines. Estimates in this regard have been in the range of 15 to 22 million mentally handicaps. Some of the studies are well systematized and conducted on fairly large samples. Gupta and Sethi (1970) screened 1500 families, of which 1000 were urban and rest rural. A total of 8583 individuals (5892 urban and 2691 rural) constituted the sample. The prevalence figures for the rural population was 2.53 per cent and for the urban 1.85 per cent resulting in an overall prevalence of 2.33 per cent. Narayanan (1981) in a study of 10,700 individuals reported prevalence figures of severe retardation (I Q 50-25) to be 0.34 per cent. Subramany (1983) using a simple questionnaire for 1498 children in the age group of 3-14 years, found an incidence of 2.7 per cent with a 2 : 1 male female ratio. Thus, no reliable statistics are available, mostly due to the lack of finances and personels. From the reports of WHO (1968) the prevalence has been assessed to be around 3 per cent of 24 million people. When this figure is added to the 48 million parents of mentally retarded persons, the problem is characteristic of one out of every eight individuals.

According to the WHO figures, in most of the countries including India, 1 per cent of the population suffers from severely incapaciting mental disorders and 10 per cent from mild mental disorders. That is, to say in India, there could be six to seven million severly mentally ill people and ten times more than that number (60 to 70 million) are mildly ill persons.

The present world population of mentally handicapped is approximately 4400 million and out of this only 38 per cent or 1672 million are children under the age of 15 years. Approximately one quarter of the World's population live in the developed countries while the remaining reside in the developing countries. India alone accounts for more than 500 million of these children. According to another study done by Seeta Sinclair, mentally retarded children comprise 3 to 5 per cent of the general population. This is a common condition. There are many such children. Most studies from many countries show a prevalence of 2 to 3 per cent of mental handicap in the general population i.e. of an I Q below 70. The majority of, about 75 per cent of such cases are mildly handicapped while the minority of 25 per cent of the handicapped, or 40 per thousand of the general population are moderately handicapped i.e. with an I Q below 50.

Gangrade (1989) asserted that adequate attention has not been given to mental problems and their related services in India. The first attempt in this direction was made by drawing a comprehensive document entitled 'National Mental Health Programm' for India in 1982. The document stated that about 10 million citizens of India are affected by mental disorders; the figures for neurosis and psychosomatic disorders are about 2 to 3 times higher thus, indicating that 20 to 30 million may require our attention. Mental ratardation is estimated at 0.5 to 1.0 per cent of all children while alcohol and drug dependence rates though still low as compared to the world scene, reveal disturbing trends in some pockets. The document further mentions that the number of cases of serious mental disorders which become manifest each year can be estimated to be roughly 35 per 1,00,000 or about 25,000 in the country. With the methods of treatment and prevention available in modern health care, chronicity and disability can be avoided in about 50 per cent of the cases. Complete and lasting recovery is possible in no less than 60 per cent. Though reliable data are not available yet there is evidence to show that learning and behaviour problems may be found amongst 1 to 2 per cent of school going children. Similarly, psychiatric problems among older people especially in the large urban areas are assuming importance due to weakening of the traditional family structure and social support system.

Problems of Mentally Retarded Children

The mentally handicapped children are capable of development and this capability is more easily developed, when a child enters an educational programme at the early stage. It is, thus, of great importance to diagnose an affected child at an early stage as far as possible. Newer techniques of early stimulation, conditioning and behaviour modification not only give the mentally handicapped the best possible chance of near normal development but also prevent the secondary psychological problems of maladjustment and behavioural disturbances due to mishandling such children. Educational facilities need to be developed on a wider scale in a large country. No large scale programme for the education, welfare and rehabilitation of the mentally retarded can succeed without broad-based community involvement.

These children, however, deviate intellectually so significantly from the normal that provision of a special class has been found to be the best educational placement for them. They are educable and this fact had been recognized by majority of the States, In these states the State Department of Education usually encourages local communities to make special class provisions for the mentally handicapped by providing supplementary funds for their support.

The mentally handicapped can learn the basic academic fundamentals and can learn to use and apply these skills in situations in which they are needed. In addition, mentally handicapped children have the potential of becoming adequately social and economic members of society. They can learn to get along in the community independently, to travel about the community and to support themselves by obtaining and holding jobs.

Chapter 5

AMELIORATION OF THE MENTALLY HANDICAPPED CHILDREN

THE human mind is a fundamental resource for development. If development has to have any purposeful meaning, quality of life must be improved and in this process, the handicapped population, including the mentally retarded, must have opportunities for leading as normal a life as is possible. Few people realize the anguish the mental retardation causes, both to those afflicted and to their families. Lack of awareness is colossal and dawnting. In these turbulent and troubled times, it is difficult to be optimistic but the initiative taken to educate mentally handicapped children displays a silver lining in the clouds.

Brief History

It has been a big problem to educate and train the mentally handicapped human beings from the ancient times. Instead of improving their behaviour and bringing them to the level of average person, they were isolated and there are references in literature which show that such persons were even persecuted. The scientific study and special supervision of the mentally deficient or mentally retarded began at the turn of the nineteenth century, with the capture of a wild boy of Aveyron. Jean Marc Gaspard Itard (1775 to 1839), a French Physician and Otologist undertook the training of this boy in order to demonstrate the influence of physiological education. Although the results of this experiment were relatively not very encouraging but set a pattern of educational therapy. The subsequent efforts of Adoured Seguin (1812 to 1880) led to a systematic interest in the study, treatment and disposition of the feebleminded. Later on, Maria Montessori (1870 to 1952), an Italian pediatrician who became an educationist, took great interest in their education and invented a unique method of training young mentally retarded and culturally deprived children. This paved the way for the development of the mentally retarded persons on modern scientific lines. As a result, various remedial measures comprising of psychological and clinical methods for imparting education and training to make them better adjusted to the society, have been devised.

Special Education

If mental retardation is considered a significant deficit in learning aptitude or potential, coupled with impaired cognitive or motor ability, then it is obvious that the handicap involves practically the whole human system. Consequently, every relevant discipline should be involved in the identification, treatment and rehabilitation of the mentally handicapped.

Mentally handicapped children whose damage is moderate or severe, require the following types of services.

1. Early detection and intervention.
2. Special schools or special classes in ordinary schools.
3. Ancillary services like physiotherapy, occupational therapy, speech therapy etc.

Handicapped children may vary so much from the normal that the regular schools can not take care of them. They can not profitably attend the schools and seldom have an adjustment with the regular curriculum which could benefit them. It is only possible for this group of children to be educated properly by providing special education to them.

At a meeting held in 1968 under the UNESCO auspices, a group of consultants defined Special Education as, "An enriched form of general education aimed at enhancing the quality of the lives of those who labour under a variety of handicapping conditions; enriched in so far as it makes use of specially trained education personnels who are aware of the application of methodological equipment to effect certain types of handicap. In the absence of such intervention, many of the handicapped are likely to suffer a degree of social incompetence and inadequacy and to live well below the level of their potentials." This definition though brief and generalized distills the essence of special education.

The promise underlying this definition is that all children are entitled to an education which will help them to utilize their capabilities. It does not require much imagination to realize that any disability, be it emotional, socio-economic, physical, sensorial or intellectual will prevent a child from much needed experiences and will consequently adversely affect the course of its developmental growth. If a handicapped child is to be helped to develop to an optimal level, appropriate experiences must be provided creatively and artistically with the utilization of special skills and sound theory on the part of the teacher. It is these special skills and sound theoretical information which distinguish the special educators from teachers. The special educator should have the ability and skills to work with the handicapped individuals. Though the pivotal factor for a good special education programme is the competent special educator, it must be remembered that for optimal learning on the part of the child, an inter-disciplinary team service will be required to tackle various problems of a syndrome of which mental handicap is just one symptom.

Objectives of Special Education

These objectives can be stated in terms of the performance or development expected of a child after the lapse of either a certain number of years of life or years spent with a programme. There is difference in our expectations from a normal child with normal abilities and a mentally handicapped child with abilities similar to those of a young normal child. The reason is the behaviour, which must only be determined by the level of ability but also by the expectations of society. Societal norms can not be flouted if the mentally handicapped individual is to be a fully accepted member of that society. This disparity in the behaviour related to ability and behaviour expected by society is widest with other children and with a greater severity of handicap. Because of these problems, objectives must take into account both chronological and mental age. The special educator will have to derive the specific detailed objectives for each child to attain the broadly stated goals for all levels of mental handicap, the profoundly, servely, moderately and mildly mentally handicapped. At this juncture, the challenge to educate the handicapped children has become apparent. This challenge makes itself felt in three ways i.e. educationally, socially and individually.

Educationally, the challenge is far greater than just that of properly educating the handicapped. It calls attention to our responsibility for providing the best possible setting for educating them. They must be given special help and attention. This special help involves, (i) individual instruction, and (ii) preparation of special material.

Social challenge of such education has two aspects, one relates to the social well-being and the other to the financial support. Socially, this group has to be trained in such a manner that they develop habits which are socially acceptable and are in accordance with the social norms. They can also be trained to become self-supporting.

Individually, this challenge is more impressive. Mentally handicapped children develop self-confidence as long as they are members of a special education class group. They are trained to accept failures. A programme of special education provides the child with work that he can do. He is permitted the 'feel of something accomplished'. The programme of special education substitutes the development of any capacity that the child may have. He is thus, educated and trained to be self-supporting. The realization of ability to support himself brings to the child, a feeling of freedom which in turn begets self-confidence.

Grouping

Children in school should be grouped on the basis of similarity of characteristics and similarity of educational needs. Within each class-room, children should be grouped as homogenously as possible with regard to their educational needs. Since, there is nothing sacred or permanent about a group, as a child's educational needs change, the composition of the group with whom he is placed also changes. Slow learners should be placed in an educational setting that is designed in terms of each child's characteristics, background, experiences and level of development. Grouping of all children on this basis will tend to group slow learners together.

Slow learners should be integrated with other children for those activities which they can perform on a relatively equal basis. Since, the slow learners'abilities are primarily in the verbal and intellectual area, the possibility of many of them participating with normal children in art, music, industrial arts, home making and physical education is very good. The probability that effective integration can be accomplished in the skill and academic subject areas is highly questionable.

Many modern educators object to the homogenous grouping, primarily on a social basis, stating that this method deprives children from having the opportunity to associate with all other children. This is understandable as it is an unnatural life situation which gives bright and average children no opportunity to learn to understand slow learner children and appreciate the contribution they can make. It also provides the slow-learners with an opporunity to appreciate this relative relationship with bright children or to benefit from the intellectual stimulation they provide. Furthermore, the classes with the slow-learner children often have a stigma attached to them thus, destroying much of the value they may have. The attitudes of the children hurdled in these classes towards themselves and the attitudes of other children towards them all act negatively.

The slow-learners compose the largest group of mentally retarded persons. Among the general school population, 15 to 17 or 18 per cent of the children can be considered slow learners. Since they are in a very large group and they do not deviate as markedly from the average as do the other groups of mentally retarded children, special educational provisions have not been considered essential. They do provide one of the largest and most intense, continuing problems being faced by the general classroom teacher.

Numerous types of problems and specific behaviourisms have been attributed to the slow learners, based on the hearsay evidence and unscientific observations of a few naive or biased observers. The slow learners have been victims of a great deal of misconceptions and misinformation regarding their characteristics and educational problems. Basically, the slow learners seen in the public schools are children with similar physical, intellectual, educational and emotional characteristics as most of the normal children have. Their general appearance and reactions are much the same as those of children in general. It is impossible to distinguish them from others by merely looking at them or even by giving them a thorough physical examination. This is probably the cause of many of their difficulties—they appear to be so 'normal', so average. Consequently, the casual observer and the unaware educator do not recognize or realize their deviations and the resulting problems.

Large individual differences in children create serious problems of psychological, educational, social and ethico-civic adjustment that they can be effectively coped with only by differentiated and individualized education and treatment.

Curricular adjustments to meet individual requirements, may take as flexible promotion plans, trial promotion, multiple curriculum, adjusted programmes in the regular school grades, individualized instruction programmes, ability sanctioning and special classes. The programme for slow learners differ the least from that provided to normal children. The special education subject areas are termed as "Adjunctive Therapies", since the main objective of the special subjects are therapeutic functions. Art, physical education, music, role playing etc. have been identified as special subject areas and a part of adjunctive therapies.

Adjunctive Therapies

The term 'adjunctive' when applied to therapeutic procedures, may be construed as having two meanings. On one hand, it may refer to media that are used as auxillaries or aids to other treatment or counselling activities. Thus, artisitc activities such as drawing or finger painting may be utilized as non-verbal psychotherapeutic techniques. Art provides a medium through which an individual of limited expressive ability may give vent to feelings and ideas without having to put them into words. Robinson and Robinson (1965) indicated that 'a number of workers have utilized artisitic media as adjunct to psychotherapy with both retarded adults and retarded children.' By the same token music has been described as an adjunct medium by Hadley (1958) who reported that music often provides an opening wedge to help the counsellor, to gain support with the client.

The use of recreational activities in a psychotherapeutic relationship may play a role in facilitating the therapist-client interaction. DeMartino (1957) characterizes recreational therapy as a psychotherapeutic approach through which the therapist has an additional opportunity to impart "basic need gratification" which DeMartino suggested is one of the chief avenues through which therapy occurs, particularly among institutionalized retardates.

Under the second meaning of the term, adjunctive therapies, are the adjustment techniques, that, as part of an overall institutional programme, are designed to effect positive behavioural changes yet these techniques do not always fit under the aegis of such recognized 'therapeutic' departments as medicine (including psychiatry), psychology and social services. A department of adjunctive therapy may include sections on recreational therapy, occupational therapy, music therapy and art therapy. Ideally, each of these sections which may function as autonomous departments in some settings, is under the direction of an individual with specialized training in the respective field. The point to be noted here is that psychological training is not a prerequisite in filling these positions or conducting these programmes. The important variable is a level of technical skill on the part of the staff member in his own area of specialization, and the ability to provide the resident with the means through which his sense of well-being, his behavioural effectiveness, and his social relationships may be enhanced without psychotherapeutic intervention.

Another important difference between adjunctive therapies and psychological therapies is that, the latter are extended only to those children who are diagnosed as needing them while the former may in many instances be extended to all residents. This is particularly true of recreational activities and, to lesser degree, of art, music and occupational activities. The resident does not necessarily have to manifest "maladjusted" behaviour before he is included in these therapeutic programmes.

While psychological training on the part of therapist and maladjustment on the part of the resident are not necessarily requisite for conducting an adjunctive therapy programme, it is contended that the various activities contribute to positive behavioural changes or social and emotional adjustments. Towards that end the following activities are advanced.

Art Activities

When the artistic media are employed as non-verbal psychotherapeutic techniques, the lable 'art therapy' might be appropriate King (1954), Freeman (1956) and Kadis (1957). However, the term 'Art Activities' programme seems more meaningful and less equivocal when such media as drawing, painting, or finger painting are employed as part of a large scale recreational programme under the supervision of a (non-psychologically) trained person. The goal here is to improve an individual's adjustment by giving him interesting and creative tasks through which he might be able to (i) express himself,(ii) gain a feeling of accomplishment, (iii) develop his talent, or (iv) enhance his general feeling of well-being.

The programme for slow learners differs the least from that provided to normal children in the special subjects areas- arts, music and physical education while the great artist and great musician must have superior intelligence, slow learners are sufficiently intelligent and close enough to the average to be able to both, enjoy and perform creditably in these areas. Much of the art activity should be related to the unit activities in which the children and class are engaged. Other art activities are for fun, related to holidays and for the purpose of learning techniques to improve communication and expression, these two should also be included.

Physical Education

Physical education is important for slow learners. It should include formal exercises as well as games or recreational activities. With generally poor physical and motor abilities, they need to develop these skills at least to the point where they will be able to perform adequately. Formal exercise is good for correction and physical development as well as for improvement of motor skills. However, this must be accomplished by games and recreational activities, for only in this way, will these abilities be put to use not only in school but also in the children's out of school activities. Major emphasis should be placed upon the kinds of activities that persons in the community can do and participate in. Examples of such activities are swimming, golf, tennis, baseball etc. depending upon the facilities available. These programmes provide innumerable experiences of value to the slow learners. Participation in all these activities give an opportunity for the children to learn school skills and to understand their necessity and value. Athletics, clubs, school plays etc. can help to broaden and enrich the individual's knowledge of the surrounding.

Occupational Therapy

The American Association on Mental Deficiency Manual for state institutions defines occupational therapy as medically prescribed and professionally guided or physical or mental activity devised to treat specific disorders or disabilities. This broad statement which could very easily be applied to a number of other therapeutic procedures is then further qualified. In mental retardation, occupational therapy may be especially valuable in the treatment of residents manifesting physical disabilities, emotional disturbances and wide variety of perceptual handicaps.

Flaherty (1956) provides a conscise definitional statement that distinguishes this technique from others: 'In any field of service, occupational therapy is treatment by means of participation in the occupations or activities devised for a specific problem.' Hutt and Gibby (1958) in describing occupational therapy as a therapeutic approach with the retarded child, indicated that this approach involves creative activity on the part of the retarded child such as simple wood working, clay modelling, weaving and the like. Occupational therapy enables the child to develop his interests and aptitudes and provides a means through which specific disabilities may be corrected.

Soper (1946 and 1957) holds the view that for the institutionalized mentally retarded, occupational therapy is essentially a "teaching behaviour" designed to instil patterns of utilizing such media as art and crafts, music, games and recreational activities. However, he further noted that occupational therapy must be prescribed by a staff physician before a resident is enrolled in such a programme.

Recreational Services

The term—recreational connotes those activities that are used for fun, recreation, profitable use of leisure time, or entertainment. Another definition of recreation might be — "any form of leisure time experience or activity in which an individual engages himself because of the enjoyment and satisfaction it brings to him".

The term 'recreational therapy' is often loosely applied to such services that are rendered to the mentally retarded in the institution or the community. Though the therapeutic role of recreational activities have not been fully established but it has been observed that recreation programming should provide each resident with enjoyable leisure-time activities through interesting and worthwhile recreational persuits.

Recently there has been recognition of the need for amelioration services for the 5 to 6 million mentally retarded children and adults in our population today. Of this number, more than 95 per cent live as independent or semi-independent individuals in their home-communities. Most recreational agencies are not available to them and so it is necessary for their families to provide them with social and recreational activities.

In 1962, a special conference on Recreation for Mentally Retarded Children was held at Teachers' College, Columbia University, co-sponsored by Comeback Inc. and the National Association for Retarded Children. In the following year, two workshops in recreation programming for the retarded were held at Columbia. It was found that among these mildly retarded individuals who were employable in certain types of jobs, a major problem had been to develop social competence and constructive use of leisure time. Experiments in recreation services are being carried on in vocational training centres for such adolescents and young adults. Such programmes whether their purpose be to improve vocational competence, develop potential abilities or simply improve the quality of living for a group that too often has been condemned to a barren and hopeless kind of existence, provide a challenge that can not be ignored by thoughtful citizens.

Purpose of Leisure Education

The chief purpose of leisure education, in any form of education, is to bring about certain desirable changes in the students who are exposed to it. These changes may be stated in terms of (i) attitudes, (ii) knowledge, (iii) skills, and (iv) behaviour.

(i) Attitudes

It is essential that students develop awareness of the importance of leisure in society and a recognition of the significant values that it may contribute to their lives. Coupled with this should be, favourable attitudes, leading to direct personal involvement in a variety of enriching and satisfying activities. Certainly, the exact nature of these activities is a matter of individual choice, it may be that in some cases, they will be within a fairly narrow and intense range of interest. Essential tool is the inculcation of a keen sense of taste and discrimination, and the ability to make sound judgement and rational choices with respect to all kinds of leisure participation.

(ii) Knowledge

Sound attitudes must be supplemented by knowledge about the 'how','why' and 'where' of recreational participation through direct experience and exposure, the student learns about recreational opportunities on many levels and comes to realize how he may become involved in them, and what kinds of outcomes may be derived. He gains information about recreation resources in the community, and learns to make full use of them. In all forms of society, there is much specific information, beyond mere physical skill that underlies successful participation.

(iii) Skills

The purpose of teaching skills is not to have a student master a number of specific activities with the thought that he will necessarily participate in them at the core of his recreational life in later years and adulthood. It is, rather to provide him with certain basic skills directly related to recreational opportunities presently available so that he may participate in these activities with a degree of competence, success and pleasure. It is difficult to predict whether he will participate in the same activities years later. Certain activities may not appeal to him as an adult, or may not be available in his community. It is also true that fads come and go in terms of recreational participation.

However, if there is effective instruction in a group of widely available activities and pastime that have been consistently popular among people of all ages, it is likely that there will be a carry over of participation.

(iv) Behaviour

Each of the preceding goals (attitudes, knowledge and skills) lead to this ultimate purpose. The outcome of leisure education must be good behaviour, which is marked by good judgement in the selection of recreational persuits; a diversity of leisure interests that meet physical, emotional and social needs and social competence in participation. This means that the school has a responsibility to provide a laboratory experience, either by directly sponsoring or by co-operating with other community agencies that do sponsor recreational programmes that implement its programme of leisure education. The teaching effort of the school is meaningless if it does not lead to real participation of the students. Only then can behavioural changes be confirmed, with habits of effective participation.

Psychotherapy

This broadly refers to effective behavioural or personality changes in the direction of more effective adjustment through planned pyschological, as opposed to medical means. This term may only be applied legitimately to therapeutic procedures employed by psychiatrists and psychologists.

Psychotherapy may be defined as the systematic utilization of pyschological techniques, chief of which is a close interpersonal relationship, by a professionally trained therapist in order to help individuals who need or seek his assistance in the amelioration of their emotional or behavioural problems. The procedure may include non-verbal as well as verbal techniques, and the subjects may or may not be aware of the dynamics of the therapeutic process.

Objectives

The major goals of psychotherapeutic efforts toward the mentally retarded fall into three principal categories: i) changes in the I Q level, ii) emotional or behavioural adjustment and iii) milieu or environmental modification.

i) Changes in the I Q Level

The psychotherapeutic objectives of changes in the I Q referred to attempts at reversing, or 'curing' the condition by raising the level of measured intelligence significantly, thus removing the 'fundamental cause' of the retardation. Under this objective, effectiveness of the treatment was gauged by the extent to which test scores rose from pre to post-treatment.

ii) Emotional or Behavioural Adjustment

It is primarily psychological treatment applied with a certain amount of regularity and consistency. The chief medium through which the psychological treatment is affected is a close and many a times emotional relationship between the subject, primarily referred to as either patient or 'client' and the therapist. However, in some cases, as with the schizophrenic child who can not tolerate close interpersonal contact, the technique may require the deliberate maintenance of a relationship that is more distant.

It requires an adequate level of preparation and training on the part of the therapist that provides him with the tools, the critical background and the practical experience, with which to treat the emotional or behavioural problems.

Psychotherapy may be effective either in an individual or group setting. Individuals in need of psychotherapy often seek this assistance, however, other individuals who need therapy but do not seek it (e.g. young children and many mentally retarded individuals) must be referred in one way or another.

The amelioration of the problems requiring psychotherapy may be carried out through verbal or non-verbal procedures (play and activity media).

Since children may very often be unaware that they are undergoing a personality reorganization, need not necessarily be the goal of all psychotherapeutic relationships. Awareness on the part of the subject is not seen as a necessity to the present definition.

iii) Milieu or Environmental Modification

It is not a medical treatment in the sense of utilizing drugs and other medication. Thus, its practice is not necessarily limited to any given profession. Psychotherapy is generally accepted as part of the reportoire of the psychiatrist, psychoanalyst and clinical psychologist. Psychological intervention is a form of drugless therapy and not subject to restriction of licensure. Of course, some sort of regulatory or supervisory procedure is necessary to ensure that only those individuals who are properly qualified through training and experience are permitted to function as pyschotherapists.

Psychotherapy does not include any type of physical treatment, including speech therapy, although the latter may be used in conjunction with psychotherapy in those cases where the speech disorder reflects emotional problems.

Teaching procedures and guidance activities that are primarily oriented toward information dissemination and advice-giving are not considered psychotherapeutic.

There is some general disagreement over whether procedures involving environmental modification and subsummed under such labels as "milieu therapy" or "environmental therapy" may legitimately be designated as psychotherapy.

Researches in the areas of mental handicap, exceptionality and intelligence have revealed very significant vivid pattern on the continuum of intelligence. This insight, though obvious, deserved quantification as well as experimental support. In a series of experiments (Mohan and Jain, 1979, 1983; Mohan and Bajaj, 1984, 1985; Mohan and Bhatia, 1985) attempted to quantify the differences among mentally retarded, normal and gifted children on simple and choice reaction time, tapping, backward figure writing, signal detection, and fluctuation of attention using standard procedure 60 Ss i.e. 20 mentally retarded, 20 normal and 20 gifted children were individually tested. It was found that the differences in simple reaction time were amplified in choice reaction time showing clearly the effect of intelligence. On both, psycho-motor tasks and tests of vigilance, the gifted children performed the best followed by the normal and the retarded. However, on the fluctuation of attention test, no significant differences were observed.

Play Therapy

Play is the child's easiest and most natural medium of self-expression and an outlet for expressing his feelings which he can not otherwise express. Clinical psychologists have experimented extensively with play therapy as a method useful for diagonising and treating children who have grave emotional problems and personality disturbances. In play therapy, the ability of the pre-school child to employ toys and dramatic play as a medium for expressing his fantasy life is utilized. For example, a play situation is arranged in which dolls represent the several members of the child's family. The child is asked to tell something about the dolls or to do something with them. In other case, he may be requested to complete a partly finished story pertaining to the dolls or to interpret a picture.

The purpose here is to provide a means whereby the young child may indirectly and perhaps unwittingly reveals his real attitude towards the members of his own family or towards others. In employing this technique, the therapist tries to create a permissive atmosphere which will encourage the child to express his deepest feelings, either by means of words or gestures, movements, clay modelling, finger painting etc. The proponents of such therapy maintain that the child's play often gives insight into family situations which can be obtained by no other means. They also report that the psychotherapy often dissipates the child's unconscious conflicts and improves his self-expression, thus, leading to better personal adjustment.

Play therapy has also been employed for understanding and helping children who have reading problems. Investigators even reported that for children suffering from severe emotional conflicts, significant increases in Intelligence Test Scores were obtained as result of play therapy. The explanation offered for this increase was that the play therapy frees children from their emotional problems, resulting in the children to employ their capacities more freely and adequately.

Smilansky (1953) working with the mentally retarded children found that there were significant improvements in the adjustment rating and acting out more of their aggression with the help of group play therapy. But there was no difference in the Intelligence Quotient, in general, of the two groups.

Extra-Curricular Activities

The extra-curricular programme of the school is very important for the slow-learners. It is an opportunity of providing them with numerous experiences that can not be given to them in their regular curriculum. Slow-learners should be encouraged and helped to participate in those activities so far as possible. They should attend to athletic events and school dances on the same basis as any other student enrolled in the school.

Dramatic clubs and school plays may provide an outlet for slow-learners. It is not always necessary to have dramatic talent to become a valued member of one of these groups.

Another school activity may be, the membership of one or more of the school musical organisations; choruses, orchestra, bands etc. Membership to various clubs particularly of a recreational nature, should be encouraged in those areas in which slow-learners can participate on relatively equal terms. These activities provide them opportunities to learn valuable leisure-time skills, give them important social skills and help them (as well as the rest of the students) to feel that they are a part of the school community, in much the same way that the school tries to teach them to accept themselves as a responsible part of the greater community in which they live.

Music as a Special Subject

The slow-learners are by definition, somewhat retarded intellectually as compared to normal children. Since the language, arts, arithmetic, science and social studies programmes are primarily concerned with and dependent upon skills and concepts highly correlated with verbal intelligence. It is in these areas that they deviate most widely from the normal and are faced with their major frustrations and failures. The special subject areas of the school, industrial arts, home-making, art, music and physical education are much less dependent upon high verbal intelligence. Many slow-learners can participate on a more, nearly equal footing in these areas. Broadly speaking, the educational experiences planned for and provided to slow-learners in these areas can often be quite similar to those provided normally at the elementary and secondary school levels. Moreover, many of the slow-learners can be integrated into regular special subjects classes because the criteria of relatively equal ability and participation can be satisfied.

When one discusses the need for unique kinds of learning experiences required by certain children, the image, that is immediately found in the mind of the reader or listener is the self-contained classroom. He seems to think that special curriculum and experiences can be provided only in this manner. The special subjects areas are excellent proof that this notion, even under present school organization and structure, need not necessarily be true. In actual practice, many experiences needed by the children in related special areas may be able to be provided more effectively and efficiently in ways different from special self-contained classes.

The school programmes in relation to the special subjects include physical education, art and music in most of the primary and secondary school programmes. Physical education, art and music teachers or supervisors are an integral part of most of the larger and many of the smaller school programmes. Two approaches to instructions in the special subjects are commonly found. In one case, supervisors have developed courses of study and curriculum guides (often including instructional suggestions) to be used by the class-room teacher. The daily schedule has specific times set aside for instruction when the special teacher can be present to work with the class.

In order to provide appropriate kinds of educational experiences for the children, teachers of slow-learners must have an understanding of their characteristics and their educational needs. Basically, the concept that must be kept in mind while one is planning for slow-learners is that, although they may be able to perform quite normally in so far as their physical and motor development is concerned yet they may not be able to grasp the intellectual requirements essential to adequate performance. Also, it is probable that a greater incidence of below average physical and motor development conditions will be present among the slow learners than among normal children.

The art and music programme for maximum value should be more closely integrated with the academic programme or experience unit than is usually true. Good music appreciation and vocal programmes have the same values for slow learners as they have for normal children. The music period, is not a time to play or sleep, it may be a time to relax, but above all, it is time to enjoy and learn. Like the art programme, it should not be left solely to the class-room teacher. The music teacher or supervisor should include the slow learners in the total school music programme. The one area that may present some difficulty is, learning musical notes and scale of singing at the same age level as normal children. These skills can be learned by slow learners but often it must be at a later stage. Similarly, they can also learn harmony and part singing.

Many schools have provided instrumental instruction at the elementary level of school. Large number of slow learners can and do play instruments. They should be encouraged to participate in the progamme, again and again on the same basis as normal children. Because majority of the slow learners come from homes where the income is limited and sporodic, it will probably be necessary for the schools to provide a larger percentage of the instruments than is usually needed.

Schools often provide or are provided with community musical experiences and all these experiences have value in so far as the child is ready for them, the slow learners should be presented with selected musical experiences. Forced attendance at musical events usually does more harm than good.

Slow-learners should participate in the school programmes in the same way as any other child. They should be encouraged to try out for choruses, bands and orchestras. While vocational outlets are somewhat limited in the music area, some slow learners will develop sufficient skill to perform with dance bands. The music programmes for most of the slow learners will be for appreciation or enjoyment, recreation and the opportunity to participate in all school activities, thus helping them to feel that they are an integral part of the total student body.

Music Activities

Procedures involving musical instruments, songs rhythm and musical games may be put under two categories; i) they may be recreational, (when used for fun, relaxation, profitable use of leisure time or entertainment) and ii) they may be therapeutic i.e. designed to treat pathological behaviour that may or may not be applicable to other forms of therapy. According to Longmore and Kotter (1963), activities falling under both these categories may be within the perview of an adjunctive therapy, and both are very often administered or supervised by a qualified staff member who is identified as a music therapist (a person engaged in the application of music as a rehabilitation or treatment method).

Schlotter and Sverdson (1959) suggested that recreational programmes for the mentally retarded, typically should include musical activities that are designed to effect positive behavioural changes along the same lines as those propounded for an art activity programme. However, music therapy involves a planned approach by a trained person directed towards one or more individuals with a view to modify specific maladaptive or pathological behaviour through the use of musical technique. Joseph and Heimlich (1959), Weigh (1959) Heimlich (1960), Nordoff and Robbin (1965), are also of the same view and support the use of music activities as adjunctive therapies.

Probably only second to physical education in terms of its potentials for leisure education is the elementary school music programme. So popular is music in its many forms for both children and adults, either within one's private recreational life or as part of organized community recreation programme, that the connection is obvious. Typically, community recreation programmes may include formal instruction classes, small ensembles, bands and orchestras, choruses, musical shows, community singing and participation. In addition to active participation, of course, there is a wide variety of opportunities to listen to and appreciate music, ranging from popular dance music and folk music, selections of semi-classical or serious symphonic works.

Mursell (1953) stressed that the major purpose of school music education programme is to provide young people with a means of recreation which can last throughout their lives. Describing the kinds of musical recreation carried on in the past, he observed that it gave them a sense of relaxation, renewal and togetherness which is perfectly summed up in the literal meaning of the word recreation. Thus, it would be a great mistake not to give very serious and realistic need to the leisure time uses of the art.

While accepting this point, Swanson (1961) stressed that the greater values of music can never be realized if it is experienced only on a childhood fun level. She wrote, "In presenting music as an immediate source of enjoyment, many teachers find themselves unable to develop a long range programme that assures growth in skills and insights. Pleasure and satisfaction in the use of music in a creative capacity throughout life is dependent upon the development of musical skills to a functional level. If the simple approach remains the only level of contact, boys and girls are deprived of the opportunity to grow into a more mature relationship with music."

However, if the music activity is not perceived with a strong sense of pleasure and self-reward, children are likely to be successful neither in the learning of musical skills nor in their recreational applications. An additional point is that, for many adults, it may not be feasible to be involved in actual music making; great pleasure, however, may be derived from listening to music, going to concerts and other musical events, or having a hi-fi lobby. The teaching of performing skills must be accompanied by what Swanson calls the need of the school to 'build in each child, a the capacity for response to art forms so that his life will have more richness and depth.'

Chapter 6

MUSIC THERAPY

MUSIC has frequently been used as a therapeutic agent from the ancient times. People in the villages or having rural background in the developed and the under-developed countries still believe in the chrismatic power of music for curing certain diseases and correcting physical and mental disorders of the human beings, since in almost every country or society there are saints, priests, witch doctors, magicians etc. who practice this art. Thus, with pride, music therapy points to a tradition as old as mankind itself.

The therapeutic values of music have been recognized and employed from a very early stage in the history of mankind and medicine. Its use has been reported even before the discovery of anaesthetics and analagestics (pain killers) which is evident from the fact that in olden days in Egypt and some African countries, music was used as a diversion for endurance of labour pain in women.

Historical sources verify the very existence and effectiveness of the combination of music and medicine to cure certain diseases and disorders. Classical examples are found in various countries and communities.

In Indian mythology, there are references which indicate that the *Vedic Mantras* (chants) of the *Rigveda* and the *Atharvaveda* have curative power and many diseases are cured by chanting of these *Mantras* and *Vedic Richas.* Their therapeutic effect is attributed to the fact that there are vibrations of sound at a specific level which have pronounced effects on the atmosphere and in turn affects the human beings.

King Saul's miraculous cure from depression with the blowing of harp by David is mentioned in the Old Testament. Egyptian papyri relates of priest-physicians who resorted to musical charms in treating infertility of women, and even Hower's Odyssey contained an episode testifying to the medically applicable power of music, in which he has described how a severely bleeding wound suffered by his hero Odysseus was stilled by vocal chants.

These examples bring us to an important aspect of inter-twining music, medicine, magic, and psychic or somatic response of body and mind. They also bring us to the connections between religion, cult, faith and medicine. Therapeutic techniques of medicines have been used by primitive peoples (so-called witch doctors, magicians, artists and healers) as witness to the strong influence of music on human beings. Their trade i.e. ritual would be inconceivable without music and dance, and their therapeutic acknowledgements deserve credit. At their treatment sessions, they integrate the sociological aspect which is known to play a key role in the pathogenesis and therapy of the widest variety of diseases. Healing was understood as a communal task. With that we come to a criterion that this concept may be defined as one of the major concepts of music therapy.

Concept of Music Therapy

The concept of mixing music as a part of therapy on one side with myth, superstition, cult or religion and on the other side, questioning about the placebo effects which are faced by every therapy, and finally the appeal of scientifically, under-pinning empirical facts about the concept of music therapy have forced the scientists, musicologists and physicians to put music therapy into action. Music therapy is still in its infancy. Various theories have confirmed the existence of music therapy.

Music is a unique way of expressing feelings and thoughts. It is due to its incorporation with the assimilation of different aspects of tempo, laya and metre. The tonal structure of raga weaves around a hallucinating environment in which the artist expresses his feelings in a very methodological and effective manner. Due to this power of fine expression of inner feelings in a naive and natural manner, music is considered as an important medium of therapy as any other discipline of therapy.

For the last two decades, experts of the most varied fields, primarily physicians, musicians, psychologists and musicologists have embarked on the ambitious venture of marking out the terrain of music therapy, systematizing, experimenting and altogether concentrating on setting music therapy on a solid scientific base. The difficulties encountered are inherent in the nature of the matter. Only with many reservations can the effects of music on the body and mind be quantified and qualified. Among the factors that complicate the objective assessment of these effects, the most important are differences in responsiveness to music, varying musical forms, dependence on listening habits and different intensities of effect according to active or receptive involvement with music.

Before turning to the test methods and influences that are most important for an understanding of music therapy, it should first be understood — 'what a music therapist means by the term MUSIC'. To clarify matters from the start, music as an art form is the most important link in the chain of acoustic contrivances. Equating music with 'auditory stimulus' it touches the heart of the matter. These tonal stimuli may be produced by musical instruments, as well as by electronic apparatus, everyday noises of the environment, or by the nature and the human body.

Before using music as therapy, it must be ascertained which type of music is to be used viz. composition of music, performance of music or listening to music. This is more important in the case of Western music.

Though in Western countries, music is being employed as an adjunctive therapy but has not yet been acclaimed the independent discipline of therapy but by experiments, music therapy can become a scientific style of treatment.

Therapeutic Use of Music

Music therapy can be used effectively as a prophylactic (preventive) measure and it can be used as an auxiliary to the main treatment after the onset of pathological conditions. If more awareness is created about the tonic effects of music , normal people will be inclined to try music for its therapeutic effects in their daily routine.

Music therapy is no potential rival to clinical medicine, the domain of which is diagnosis of disease. On the other hand, factors such as personal confidence relating to others, warmth, emotional expression, communication, encouragement or solace can contribute to improvement. Music therapy divests the suspicion of being an arbitrary method of treatment of diseases and as an adjunctive to the established forms of therapy, so that it may possibly balance the deficits of other methods.

The appropriate type of music helps to drive out negative feelings like dependency and loneliness. Music has a tendency to fill the mind. It creates an atmosphere of harmony and well-being. The person who is listening to, is also able to participate in the music by keeping rhythm or humming alongwith the music or even dancing to it. 'Participation therapy' is specially effective with children because it gives them a great feeling of satisfaction of being one of the group when they sing in chorus. Most children are nervous in going to school for the first time or if the school is new. The assembly-songs with which the school day starts have the requisite enthusiastic effect. Familiar tunes ease anxiety and provide reassurance as a general rule.

The music used for therapy should be selected not by the yardstick of musical excellence but with a feel for the most appropriate music for the patient's requirements. Music helps in the treatment of actual diseases in the following manner :

(i) One obvious use of music is that of a sedative. It can replace the administration of tranquilizers, or at least reduce the dosage of tranquilizers or sleeping pills.

(ii) During the treatment, music helps to divert the patient's attention from his discomfort or pain. Most people are fearful of the dentist's chair and when they come in to have their teeth extracted, the dentist finds it a great help to play music as diversionary tactics. In case of physiological trauma, as in war time, the right type of music diverts the mind of the patient from brooding on the horrors of past experience.

(iii) Music helps in making the patient more co-operative and directs his behaviour on positive lines. It is a helpful adjunct in the treatment of the maladjusted, the neurotics and others with mental and neurological problems.

(iv) Music has been found to stimulate motor activity and so it is used during physiotherapy for this purpose. Here music is not used for sedation but on the contrary, it is used to invigorate and stimulate the action of physiotherapy.

(v) Participation therapy in which the patient takes an active part, is specially good for patients suffering from anti-social feelings and general attitudes of hostility and violence towards society in general. Music, especially participation in group singing gives them the feeling of 'belonging' for which they long and they feel that they are accepted and are then able to have good personal relationships with others.

(vi) As an avenue of self-expression, music is even better than language. In repressive societies where the individual is denied the freedom to speak out and express his opinion, music can act as a safety valve.

(vii) Many teenagers need enormous amount of appreciation and applause to bolster their images. They can get this kind of adulation by performing music on stage or among friends. The great desire to be admired is thus channelized into socially accepted forms. In this form of therapy, the patient participates actively in the music.

(viii) Music when played in a room, creates a sense of security among the listeners, particularly for some patients who are afraid of either loneliness or from big gathering. Their shyness is overcome and sometimes, fear from others and unknown reasons is also eliminated.

Curative Power of Music

In many tribal cultures, percussion music is often used to direct behaviour and create appropriate moods. Rhythm is the organiser and it stimulates motor activities. Non-rhythmic music requires a longer attention span i.e. more concentration and it does not have the same excitement value.

Specific music therapy for certain disorders have been established in this field. Blowing on the horn improves abdominal muscle weakness. Playing on the cello improves the working capabilities of a polio victim. Further, piano playing improves finger co-ordination of the player and is recommended for cerebral palsy. The blind ones are helped to have a career in music and thus gain self-esteem. Deaf children are found to respond to rhythm and learn more through music therapy to control the volume of their own voice. Cripples develop co-ordination of limbs by moving them with the rhythm of music. In geriatrics, old people have a better morale when they are given regular music therapy and so they suffer less from boredom and loneliness.

Insufficient breathing, over-excitement, self-consciousness and inferiority complex are some of the causes for stammering and these are corrected by the use of participation techniques in music therapy. Spasm tensions and repeat mechanism cause stammering. Usually the problem is with the consonants. Simple rhymes and tunes facilitate the cure.

A study conducted on the correction of stammering in children with the use of music, has shown beneficial effect as there was significant effect. Speech is a psychoneuromuscular mechanism that requires a high degree of co-ordination. In case where there is no defect of the organs but only a defect in their functioning, music therapy is of great help.

Some scientists have experimented the effect of music. Dr. Vechkineski used the Chopen's symphony to cure insomania. Dr. Eving Hunter supported the results of this experiment and found that music has good effect in reducing the pain of body. Dr. Herbert Spencer experimented with people suffering from high or low blood pressure and found that fast melodies having sharp notes are effective in normalising the low blood pressure while slow melodies having soft or *Komal Swars* are helpful in lowering the blood pressure of the patient suffering from high blood pressure. A Russian scientist studied the effect of music on the physiology of human body and as a result, he concluded that music effects the blood circulation and so regulates the blood pressure. Usually heart beat increases or decreases depending upon the use of soft, flat or sharp notes and the use of fast, slow or medium tempo. He also concluded that the patient who received the music treatment showed submissive behaviour and some of them recovered fully of their diseases.

Ms. Juliet Alwin (quoted by Madhugandha, 1993) is of the opinion that music directly effects the mind, brain and body and as such its use in therapy must be done according to the state of mind of the patient. The right type of music must be used for a particular type of disease. It must also be kept in mind that the patient be provided with the desired music-equipments. For example, if he wants to use the instrument or wants to participate in solo or group performance, he should be trained properly. The patient should have some inclination towards music otherwise, it is difficult to cure him through music. The use of music is very beneficial for amelioration of mentally sub-normal children. Due to its impulsive nature, it penetrates deep into the mind and the innermost feelings are affected. Thus, music therapy is most beneficial in the case of mentally retarded cerebral palsied patients. Dr. Erwin H. Schenider experimented music therapy on 10 spastic children. He concluded that music therapy had positive effect on all types of mentally retarded children of different ages or sexes while the type of disease, type of music used and the extent to which the music was used were different variables through which he experimented music therapy.

Charles Keel and Angliki (quoted by Madhugandha, 1993) experimented music therapy with two groups of mentally retarded patients. They used Indian music on one group and Western music on the other. They chose gay, lively and cheerful *Ragas* for therapy and similar types of Western compositions. After the specific time of therapy, they found that the group who received music therapy through Indian music performed better than the patients who were subjected to Western music.

Investigations have revealed that a significantly greater incidence of delayed speech acquisition and signs of disordered early childhood development are observed when the rhythmic code is disturbed in this instance in mothers affected with cardiac dysrhythmia. One therapeutic consequence drawn from this premordial form of rhythmic influencing is familiar to all : the rhythmic rocking calm or lull a baby. Musical structural analysis of lullabies confirms the tranquilizing effect of a specific metre.

Auditory discrimination is usually improved through helping the children to distinguish the differences between sounds (amplitudes, pitch and quality). These activities are usually initiated with sound that are grossly dissimilar. As the children can make the appropriate selections indicating a grasp of the principle involved as well as the ability to make differentiations at this level, sounds are presented of a successively more similar nature requiring finer and finer auditory discriminations. Singing of rhymes and songs and listening to records and rhythms also contribute to the improvement of performance in this area.

Effect of Indian *Ragas*

There is an unexplored, highly scientific field of music therapy, that is, the effect of musical sounds and *Ragas* in curing human ailments. A number of successful experiments have been made to assess the effects of *Ragas* on human beings by playing particular combinations of sounds and also particular *Ragas*. Health cure with the help of the classical *Ragas* with their specific emotional sentiment has also been experimented.

Raga-Raginis can successfully be used for the treatment of various diseases but there is a need to prepare good musicians and doctors who are, expert in this discipline of therapy. Pandit Onkar Nath Thakur put to sleep Mussolini who was suffering from insomania. On the same lines musicians can follow these principles in using the Indian *Ragas* for the cure of insomania. Likewise, the effect of other *Ragas* have also been studied. A person whenever he listened to *Raga Kalingara*, had his heartbeat increased and he felt very upset. Likewise, whenever Raja Lakshman Prasad Singh of Mathura listened to *Raga Piloo*, he lost his self-control and used to cry and weep. These examples show that all the *Ragas* do not have the same effect on every human being. The effect depends on the level of emotional disturbances and emotional set-up of the individual. Moreover, the very nature of the *Raga* has also to be studied and kept in mind while preparing a programme of therapy using *Ragas*. A vast survey regarding the emotional level and responses of different *Ragas* has to be done before any form of *Raga* therapy is prepared.

Indian *Ragas* have been assigned different moods and sentiments and they are sung according to their respective aesthetic sentiment for creating different emotional moods in the minds of the singer and the listener. The six primary *Ragas* are said to have particular qualities, sentiments and moods as given below :

1. *Raga Hindol:* The effect of this *Raga* is to create in mind of the listener, all the sweetness and freshness of the spring season.
2. *Raga Shri:* This *Raga* effects the mind and produces the effect of calmness and silence of the day approaching the evening and darkness.

3. *Raga Megh Malhar:* The quality of this *Raga* is to produce the effect of approaching thunder-storm and rain. This *Raga* has also been found to have the power of influencing clouds in times of drought.
4. *Raga Deepak:* This *Raga* is said to be related to fire which can destroy the trees and animals, and even can light the fire and as such creates wonder/surprise.
5. *Raga Bhairav:* This *Raga* is to inspire the mind of the listener with the feeling of approaching dawn, humming insects and chirping of birds and the start of morning.
6. *Raga Kaushik:* The effects of this *Raga* on the listener are known to be grave and serene.

In the 5th century Matanga Muni described the intrinsic sentiments of *'Jatiragas'* in Brihaddeshi. According to him *Raga Bhinna Shadja* and *Raga Bhima Pancham* produce *'Vibhasta'* and *'Bhayanak Rasa'*. Similarly, in Sangit Samayasar, Acharya Parshvadev has also described the *Ragas* having their respective sentiments and moods. Sharngdev has described the sentiments of the *'Gram Ragas'* in Sangit Ratnakar and according to that, *Raga* should be sung with the application of sentiments in such a way that its specific sentiment is represented. On the basis of this concept, *Ragas* were dipicted in the *'Rag Dhyan'* and their iconography to represent the specific mood.

Efforts have been made to quantify the components of feelings aroused by Indian Classical music. Four musical excerpts consisting of twenty minute recordings on Ravi Shankar's Sitar recitals of four *Ragas* viz. *Kafi, Mishra Mand, Puriya Dhanashri* and *Rageshri* were played through a tape recorder. Students numbering 37, between the age range of 20 to 30 years acted as respondents. Osgood's Semantic differential technique was used for measuring the psychological meaning of things in music. The basic question in the mind of the researcher was "what do you think this music is like " (Virmani, 1968). The responses received from the experimental listeners are as follows :

Raga	Responses
Rageshri	Evening, Dark, Sombre, Deep
Kafi	Gaiety, Devotion, Romance, Pleasantness
Puriya Dhanashri	Physically tired, Evening, Longing, Grave, Dark, Sombre

Dr. Ambujan and her husband Dr. Raman's experimental study in the U.S. Hospitals using Carnatic *Ragas* also identified the responses as follows :

Response of the Indian Ragas

Raga	Responses
Khamas	Sensual love
Nandanmakriya	Gentleness
Neelambari	Sleep, relaxation
Hansdhwani	Exhilaration
Madhyamavati	Great aesthetic, equilibrium

Renu Kishore (1989) also took up a study on 'Feature analysis of responses to the Indian Classical music and concluded that the Indian *Ragas* have certain specified moods and thus have typical responses.

Altekar (1968) observed that *Ragas* like *Shankara, Patdeep, Hidnole* and others have proved good in bringing behavioural changes in children of 8 to 18 years of age. He also observed a significant change in the mood from irritating to normal after administration of music to them.

Some work has been carried out at the M.S.University, Baroda in India, for the correction of aggressiveness, heart aliments, mentally disturbed persons, mentally depressed and slow-learners, with the help of music, and beneficial effects of various *Ragas* like *Bihag, Kafi, Malkauns, Ramkali, Hindol, Bahar, Deshkar, Lalit* and *Jaijaiwanti* were recorded. It was observed that there was significant improvement in the conditions of such persons (Bhattacharya, 1970). Pandit Onkar Nath Thakur as reported by Tiwari (1980) had observed number of beneficial effects on human beings. A boy suffering from insomania was cured as a result of rendering of the *Raga 'Puriya'* by Pandit ji. It has been reported by Ved Mani Singh Thakur (1981) that malaria, hysteria, insomania, tuberculosis, constipation, typhoid and many other diseases can be cured through various *Ragas* like *Hindol, Marwa, Puriya, Bilawal, Tilang, Ramkali, Multani, Kalingra, Sohni, Kamod, Paraj, Todi, Bhairavi, Malkauns, Piloo, Bihag, Darbari Kahnara, Khamaj, Sorath, Adana, Megh Malhar, Asawari, Bhairav, Vrindavani Sarang, Desh* etc. Thakur (1981) reported that the effect of the *Raga Bhairavi* as observed by Pandit Ravi Shankar is quite extensive as it arouses the emotions of the listeners. Similar effects of other *Ragas* like *Adana, Darbari Kanhara, Khamaj, Purvi, Basant, Sorath, Hindol, Marva, Puriya, Tilang, Bilawal, Ramkali, Kalingra, Sohni, Kamod, Paraj, Multani, Todi, Bhairav, Malkauns, Piloo, Bahar, Rageshwari, Dhani, Bihag* and others were also studied. In recent times, Nawab of Rampur is said to have been cured of rheumatism with the rendering of the *Raga Jaijaiwanti.*

Dr. Thambe (1994) had used music therapy as an integral treatment of the holistic health therapy — with a combination of Ayurveda, Yoga and spiritualism, along with a simple food and living style. Research was carried out by playing specific *Ragas* from Hindustani Classical music for certain diseases and they proved effective in curing ailments ranging from ordinary stomach ache to menstrual disorders and serious maladies like schizophrenia and epilepsy. According to him, music worked quickly on the hormone system and cured the disease. *Raga Bhairavi* has been found effective in cases of schizophrenia. It induced good sleep and calmed down the patient, a process which was necessary to administer medicines to the patients. This *Raga* also provided relief in epilepsy cases and helped in reducing the frequency of convulsions in patients. *Raga Shivranjani* helped to improve memory and cure psychiatric diseases. *Raga Todi* helped to reduce tension and blood pressure while the combination of the *Raga Todi* and the *Raga Bhopali* had a soothing effect in cases of blood pressure. The impact of *Raga Malkauns* and the *Raga Asawari* was similar in such patients.

In Sangit Ratnakar, Acharaya Sharangdev has described the connection of *Swars* with *Chakra*, cells nerves, veins and physiological structure of human body. On the basis of these references quoted, B.M.Ledger has conducted many experiments and found these aspects effective. He observed a young child singing La La La, and in this exercise, only the ribs of the child were in action. After that the child was asked to sing Pu Pu, and then it was seen that the lower abdomen was in action. It was also observed that while singing La La La, the child was happy but while singing Pu Pu, the diaphragm and muscles were tense. After this experience, some more effects of different types of combinations of *Swars* were tried. It was concluded that these types of exercises influence the blood pressure.

In Brihaddeshi, Pandit Ahobal has described the relationship of 22 *Shrutis* of the Indian music to 22 veins of the human body. Similarly, the nature of *Vat, Pitt* and *Kaf* have been assigned to various *Ragas*. Since the *Ragas* have different nature and because of this peculiarity in nature, they have been classified in 3 groups namely, *Vat, Pitt* and *Kaf*. The effect of these *Ragas* on human body is apparaently

noted. Thus a particular *Raga* can be used as antidote for the diseases caused by *Vat, Pitt,* and *Kaf.*

In 'Sangit Makrand' Narad has quoted in the third *Pada* —

> Aayurdharamayashobudhi dan dhanayam falam labhet,
> Ragabhivriddhisantanam purnaragah prageeyate.
> ||80||
>
> Sangramrooplavanyaviraham gunakirtanam,
> Shadvenpragatvyam lakshanam gaditam yatha.
> ||81||
>
> Vyadhinashi shattanashi bhayashokvinashane,
> Vyadhidaridrayasantape vishamgrahmochane.
> ||82||
>
> Kamadambernashe ch mangalam vishsanhrite,
> Audeven pragatvyam gramshantyarthkarmani.
> ||83||

Sampurana Ragas should be sung for the benefit of long life, *Dharma* (religion/duty), strength, wisdom, wealth, good harvest, fruits, gains, profits, prosperity and children. *Shadava Raga* (having six notes) are beneficial in conquering battle, attaining beauty, youth, charm, and singing of good names and works of warriors and heros. *Audava Ragas* (having five notes) are useful for curing diseases, winning over enemies, overcoming fear and sorrow, poverty and ills, sickness and bad health. *Audava Ragas* are also useful for observing ceremonies and for the good-will and prosperity of the community. Further mention of the occasions, circumstances and different states in which specific types of *Ragas* are beneficial, has also been made.

Nada

The dynamic effects of the *Nada* have attracted many scientists and philosophers to explore its power. It is believed that whole of the universe is dominated by the power of the *Nada*. This notion may be philosophical or scientific but there is no denial about the fact, that life from birth to death revolves round that supreme power, which is the *Nada*. Five cardinal elements — air, water, earth, sky and fire are also the basis of the *Nada*. The *Nada* has the power to achieve all the three stages i.e. *Tamas, Rajas* and *Satva*. The person when comes in contact with these cardinal elements, feels a supernatural power which is possible due to the effects of the *Nada*. Though water, fire, air and earth are quite different in their basic elements yet they are coordinated with each other in such a way that they can not be distinguished apparently but the fifth element — sky is completely obscessed by the power of the *Nada*. The existence of the *Nada* is spread all over the universe. The element of density of earth is known as density of the *Nada*. The flow of water is known as expression of the *Nada* which is fluid in nature. The energy of fire is found in the power of the *Nada* which can attract the universe with its force. The velocity of air is the *Laya* of the *Nada* which can sway the mind, body and heart. And the sky is known as the *Nada* itself due to its unlimited boundaries which is also the quality of the *Nada*.

With the help of the power of the *Nada* and the special process of the use of the *Swar*, the cardinal elements can be decreased or increased. It is also possible that a new peculiar type of element can be developed with the combination of these elements. In the Indian philosophy much emphasis is given to the supreme power of the *Nada* and attracted by this supreme power, a branch of therapy has evolved which is generally known as music therapy.

This type of therapy is connected with the relationship of soul and body. Soul is supreme and is not affected by any disease whereas body is susceptible to many diseases and disorders which can be cured with the proper use of the *Nada Tatva* which is basically the sequential application of *Swar, Laya, Tala* and concentration. The effect is apparent. It is believed that the parts of the body are made up of the five cardinal elements and the correct combination of *Swar, Laya* and *Tala* can create wonders in the world of therapy.

The correct intonation and use of the *Rishabh Swar* can cure the *Vat-Shool* i.e. arthiritis. In the same manner, there is possibility of curing the diseases concerning the respiratory problems, throat and thyroid infections, the diseases connected with lungs and ribs, low or high blood pressure, heart diseases, liver disorders, piles, ulcers, stomach diseases, diahorrea, intestinal diseases, weakness, fatigue, infertility, skin diseases and various eye/sight problems with the use of correct intonation of the *Swars* and its different combinations, but all these presumptions need to be experimented on scientific lines to establish its practical use. It is earnestly required that a team of medical practioners, psychologists, philosophers and musicians should work together to establish this type of therapy which has deep roots in the Indian literature. Modern techniques, instruments and technology should be used to give it a scientific background.

In the *Samveda*, there is a long sequence of the *'Gayan Vidhan'* to cure many diseases.

In the *Bhaishaja Tatva* of Ashwani Kumaras, four types of the *Bhaishajas* have been assigned to cure different diseases. *Pavanaukas, Jallaukas, Vanuankas* and *Shabdik* are the four *Bhaishaja* and out of this the *Shabdik Bhaishajas* are types of music therapy.

In the Konark Prabha by Kraunch Muni, there is reference about the origin of the *Shabda*, the relationship of body and the *Shabda, Shabdochar* and *Raga*, and different types of *Shabda*. All these aspects of the *Shabda* in one way or the other can be used for music therapy.

In the Shabda Kautuhal, there are four thousand *Shlokas* in three chapters. In the first chapter, with the help of the *Shabda*, patient is given the *Shabdik* treatment. In second chapter, the treatment is given by playing *Veena, Tantri, Panav, Shankh, Bheri, Mridang, Manjeer, Vanshi* etc. The *Shabdik Bhaishaja* is prepared by playing these musical instruments and when the patient listens to these *Shabdik Bhaishaja* gets relieved of his diseases. For different types of diseases, different types of the *Shabdik Bhaishaja* are used. Different instruments and tones of the musical instruments and combination of different musical instruments and tones were used to cure various diseases. It has also been described that playing of which instrument is good or suited for which disease. In the third chapter, there are references about the curative power of listening to music and meditation and the *Kirtan*.

Music therapy is dependent on the style, form, speech and pronunciation of the syllabels alongwith the intensity, pitch and timbre using the *Vilambit, Madhya* and *Drut Layakaries*. Inspired by this fact Dr. B.B Gore quoted in his article "Sangit and Ayurveda" that the nature of the *Ragas* play an important role in curing many diseases. He recommended the use of the *Ragas* having the *Shrutis* of different *Jatis*. The *Raga* having *Alapini, Madanti, Rohini, Ramya Shrutis* increases the *Kaf Prakriti* (nature) and to over-power this *Prakriti*, the *Ragas* having *Raudri, Krodhi, Vajrika Shrutis* should be sung. The *Ragas* having *Rishabh Swar* as the *Vadi* is also beneficial to cure the *Kaf Prakriti* and curing weakness, fatigue and low blood pressure. Sameway, the *Vat* and *Pitt Prakirti* can be cured by singing or listening to the *Ragas* having the *Kaf Prakriti*. The *Ragas* like *Khamaj, Tilang, Des* etc. are said to have good effects in arousing the *Prakriti* of *Pitt* and *Vat*. Nothing can be said authoritatively in the absence of proven or experimented proofs. But there is no doubt in establishing the fact that the Indian *Ragas* do have effects which can pave the way in finding out the cure of many diseases and the use of Indian *Ragas* and the *Raginis* as a means of music therapy.

Music in Therapy and as Therapy

The term 'Music Therapy' may be conceptualized as consisting of two concepts : music in therapy, and music as therapy.

The primary objective of music in therapy, is to establish contact and facilitate rapport with the subject. Children who have been in constant motion may at least be temporarily quiet down and listen. In this sense, the aesthetic and rhythmic qualities of music may provide the 'opening wedge' between the therapist and client. Weigh (1959) noted the effect of functional music as a therapeutic tool in working with the mentally handicapped children.

One therapeutic consequence drawn from a primordial form of rhythmic influencing is familiar to all : the rhythmic rocking to calm or lull a baby. Other observations appear to point in the same direction, for instance, the infants exposed to sounds stimulating heart beats cried less during the first weeks of their life and gained more weight than the control group.

Indian Classical music has very successfully been used in therapy. Various *Ragas* have been found to be very effective in curing many diseases. Thus, it has opened the doors for the musicians to use classical *Ragas* in music therapy. A major advantage of music therapy is its versatility which indicates the possibility of combining it with other related forms of therapy and neighbouring disciplines. To mention a few, are musical exercises, musico therapy with its various forms like dance, rhythmic gymnastics, aerobics, eurhythics etc. painting art activities or coupling of music therapy with relaxation and recreational therapy.

Weighing the potentials and the limitations, musicotherapy is thus, found to be adjunctive and supportive to other forms of therapy and can at best replace them after a certain success in healing has been attained. As a rule, the musicotherapist is a co-therapist, and his method of treatment is ancillary method.

In considering the dimension 'Music as Therapy', therapist is not concerned with the aesthetic and mood producing qualities of a musical composition but rather with functional music i.e. the isolation and use of such basic musical elements as rhythm, harmony, melody etc. for reaching practical therapeutical goals beyond music itself.

Joseph and Heimlich (1959) considered music therapy as a specific psychotherapeutic discipline that has particular utility where other, more traditional psychotherapeutic efforts may be ineffective. In the programme described by the authors, children are selected for music therapy on the basis of a number of specific maladaptive or pathological criteria; and in addition to those choosen all show the inability to relate satisfactorily to adults or peers.

In further delineating the various aspects of music as a therapeutic tool, Joseph and Heimlich made the following observations:

1. Music provides an opportunity for immediate satisfaction by allowing the direct, safe and constructive discharge of emotion through sound.
2. Songs may serve as media of communication, providing opportunities for individual as well as group expression and allowing for expression of feelings, wishes and activities that the child often finds difficult to talk about directly.

3. Percussion instruments are useful with all children, however, they are of particular value with timid or withdrawn children since they feel safe and secure when they play on percusuion instruments.

4. Encouraging the child to paint or use chalk while listening to music, gives him an opportunity to express his feelings through another medium, with music providing the springboard for design, colour and movement on paper. Some children derive sensuous pleasure from the combination of colour and music. Other derive feelings of self-worth through production of something of value. For all, the fact that there is no correct response in this situation fosters free expression and active fantasy.

In describing techniques for the use of percussion instruments, Joseph and Heimlich (1959) noted that one way to draw a child into responsive activity is for the therapist to listen carefully to a child's random drum-beating to catch a pattern in the random beats and to pick up and carry out this pattern in a series of dynamic improvisations.

Improvisation technique is almost incidental in the programme of music therapy. Nordoff and Robbins (1965) depended almost entirely on musical improvisation in their work with individual children. The particular approach of these workers is based upon the rationals that the manner in which the child responds to improvisation yields a 'musical self-portrait' where there is detectable connection between the child's pathology or personality and this self-portrait, and the therapist can effectively utilize that relationship to give direction to his own efforts.

Working with mentally retarded children, Weigh (1959) described the use of functional music and equated it to 'music as therapy'. She indicated that the goals of this approach vary with the needs of the mentally retarded, with the major emphasis on social adaptation. Similarly, Knight, Ludwig, Strazulla and Pope (1957) described the use of functional music as a part as the remedial programme for strengthening the motor acts of hyperactive retarded children.

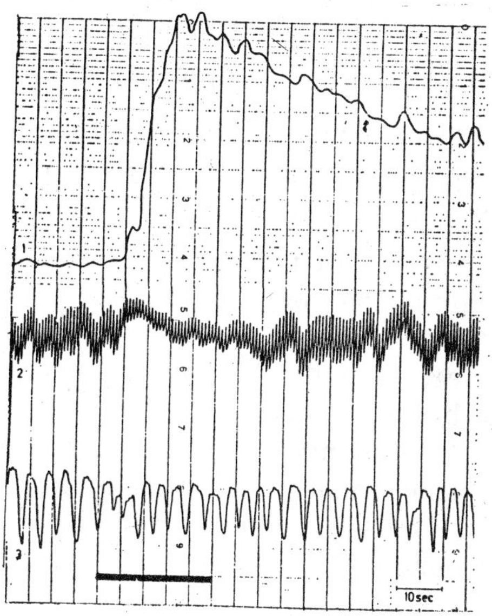

Autonomic diagram recorded under exposure to noise. 1 psychogalvanic reflex (PGR), 2 finger oscillogram, 3 respiration. Commencement of noise(■)is marked by maximum deflection of PGR, typical reduction of finger oscillogram amplitudes to about half initial value as expression of peripheral value as expression of peripheral vessel construction enduring beyond noise stimulus, and temporarily irregular breathing.

Music therapy is a technical and biological process since it involves the use of music for the human beings. Thus, it is tempting to put a phenomenon so difficult to objectivize the effect of music on human beings by taking measurements with suitable instruments. Treating the evidence with due caution, it is possible to produce an 'autonomic diagram' using instruments such as an electro-encephelograph (for assessment of amplitude and frequency of the brain waves), an electro-cardiograph (action on heart rhythm being of prime interest), a spirometer to record the rate and depth of respiration, an oscillograph and plethysmograph for interpretation of bloodflow conditions, a psychogalvanic skin reflex recorder, and an electromyograph.

The biosignals emitted by the autonomic nervous system under the influence of music, when charted, produce some useful, interesting, and curious findings.

It has been shown that music in a major key and discords quicken the heart action and increase blood pressure whereas a minor key and consonance have the opposite effect. Another example illustrates the relationship between the vein of music and specific reaction of the autonomic nervous system; in exposure to march and dance music, substantially higher electrical activities in the muscles are measured on the lower limbs than on the forehead.

The observation that the effects triggered are appreciably stronger when actively participating in music than in passive reception. Even the route by which reception takes place greatly effects the autonomic response. The effect of listening to music is much intenser over headphones than by loudspeaker. For example, functions of the mammary glands is influenced in nursing mothers when they listen through headphones, and incidentally the effect is found exclusively with classical or "pleasant" music.

It is, thus, evident that the application of music in therapy and as therapy has been proved by following various technical and scientific procedures. This will be the best use of music for the human beings.

Chapter 7

APPLICATION OF MUSIC THERAPY

In a democratic country, all children are entitled to an education which will help them to utilize their capabilities to the maximum level. It must be realized that any disability, be it emotional, socio-economic, physical, sensorial or intellectual will not prevent a child from much needed experiences. Mentally handicapped children occur in a large number in our country. These children are with sub-average intellectual functioning and substantially below the average child in learning and as such they lag behind the school schedule in their academic achievement; they also feel themselves socially insecure and unadjusted in the school and in the society.

Children, like all other human beings, have the same urges and needs for their survival and getting recognition from their fellow classmates in the school and out of school environment. According to Maslow (1954), the basic human needs to sustain and preserve life are the physiological and physical like safety and security. Once these needs are fairly well established, social needs followed by psychological needs emerge. It is only when the social needs become dominant, a child will survive for meaningful relations with others and finally the need for self-esteem and recognition from others is apt to arise, and so Maslow expressed it as "What a man can be, he must be." Different components of social and psychological needs like attainment, achievement, self-esteem etc. are supplementary to the educational needs. In order to achieve respect, prestige and recognition by others, a normal child desires to excel in educational achievements.

Thus, creating an urge for their educational needs. Mentally handicapped children pose a problem for the teacher in the regular schools for average children. They are not able to cope with the normal education programme in the school.

The aim of educational programme for the mentally handicapped children is to bring all-round development so that they may acquire social, educational and psychological adequacies and be accepted by the society. In the absence of such intervention, many of the mentally handicapped children are likely to suffer a social incompetence and inadequacy and are to live well below the level of their potential. The level of mentally handicapped children can be improved by providing them special education, may be through music as suggested by Slack (1970) who found significant improvement in the skill in the subjects of school curriculum of such students due to artistic appreciation as induced by music education.

Aims of Music Education

Music is more a subject of character development rather than that of education. Music education is for fundamental personality development and not simply the transmission of certain techniques, therefore, the aim of this education is to promote the development of creative abilities, emotionality of perception and social consciousness through aesthetic experience.

The purpose of music in education is not to produce a ready-made audience with "well informed" tastes; it is decidedly not the object to produce a market for specific goods, but is to produce a musical climate both open-minded and critical, to produce musical skills and crafts and to encourage human beings to be humane.

What music does for all of us? At its best, is to sharpen our sense of intution, while at the same time sharpening our analytical and critical faculties. Keeping this is view, probably John Howes (1903) while writing about the curriculum has said,"Children should learn to sing, to play upon all sorts of instruments, as to sound the trumpet, the cornett, the recorder or flute, to play upon shagbolts, shalms and all other instruments that are to be played upon." The idea of including music as a subject of study is dominated by the main argument in favour of music, on the one hand that music is good for the individual person and on the other hand, it is needed by the society or the community for many of its social functions such as those associated with the church, the court and with civic activities.

All power and all development come through growth. It is true for every field of human endeavour, certainly including music and as such it should be included in every kind of teaching, all the way from alphabet to higher mathematics. The developmental approach in music education means emphasizing and playing up musical varieties at all times, on all occassions and in all possible ways. Music education includes the music activities and music learning which develop the social aspect of life. It also aids in the development of sound work habits. Given an accepting and adequately stimulating family environment and appropriate vocational training facilities, the majority of the mentally retarded children can develop good social and vocational adjustment and capacity for appropriate interpersonal interactions and attachments. However, in this process, they face hazards that exceed the ones facing the normal population. Such problems seem to increase in direct proportion to the degree of retardation.

Importance of Music Education

The education of music has been regarded as an important tool for the betterment of behaviour and academic achievements of the children. Plato (428-348

B.C.) once wrote, "I would have no man a school master unless he is also a musician" because, he felt that of all the subjects in a school curriculum, music was the one truly educational subject, for it not only trains the mind but also trains and purifies the emotions. According to Copland (1952), Martin Luther (1483-1546), an accomplished musician placed great values on music education as it induces one to forget all wrath, unchastity, arrogance and other vices.

While stressing the need of music education in the life of school going children, Leonhard and House (1959) suggested that a music programme should also include singing in large and small groups with the aim of developing musical independence and the ability and desire to use music in out-of-school life. It has been reported by Nketia (1961) that music education had significant effect on the personal adjustment which gave each individual the opportunity to reach the highest level he is capable of.

Farnsworth (1967) found that application of music has different effects like bringing physiological changes, curing both physically and mentally handicapped persons, and on their achievements. The effect of music was found significant, in particular to reduce fatigue and to stimulate the depressed emotions. In another study, Paul Michel (1970) found that the music education training had developed in a person the ability to differentiate and discern, to remember, to think in musical terms, the development of musical imaginations and to help enormously in mastering difficult professions.

Hoffmann (1970) is of the view that music instruction to youth stimulate their interest in art, develop artistic taste and professional skills which contribute to development of harmonious personality. The primary Self-Concept Inventory designed by Miller and Leonetti (1973) was administered by Park (1979) who found that both, pre- and post-test observations, indicated a positive correlation between the self-concept and achievement in the moderately mentally retarded population.

Wolff (1979) studied the effect of general music education on the academic achievement and perceptual-motor development, creative thinking and school attendance and found that experimental groups achieved higher scores on creative thinking, originality and perceptual-motor development but did not have beneficial effect on school attendance, reading scores and mathematics.

Muller (1982) carried out the historical and comparative study of the role of music in child education and concluded that music has the possibility to help order aspirations, lighten burden in life, control temper and balance power ambitions with support and directs the exploration of aspiration. The role played by music in the educational programme of children becomes a share in the education of humanity.

Hanshumaker (1980) stated that music is effective in raising the level of intellectual development of the mentally retarded children. He further, holds the view that arts education positively influences the social development and the personal adjustment and such programmes are particularly effective with mental retardates and therefore, carefully planned experiences in the arts, result in unique and positive influence on critical aspects of both intellectual and social development.

Effect on Academic Achievement

Music in different forms has been used by many investigators to study its effect on the academic achievement of the children: most of them are in favour of including music in the school curriculum while there are few who have not found any significant difference between experimental and control group of pupils.

Improvement in the general achievement of young people has often been reported since children studying in general education schools with music tutions experience a richer world of moods and feelings, their musical studies help them to do better in other subjects, not only because music builds up overall tone, increases the pupils' joy of living and desire to work (Mihalyi, 1970). The improvement in writing was expressed by better handwriting which was beautiful and by accuracy in spellings. The reading ability was also enhanced as they read more frequently than their counter-parts. Further, the pupils receiving music education had a better understanding of the subjects of their study than those not receiving music education.

In the words of Erzsebet Szonyi, quoted by Sarai (1970) from an article in 'Tempo' "daily music lessons very quickly develop in small children a sense of rhythm, the technique of clear singing and expressiveness, interpretation and they train the memory and encourage accuracy". It has been suggested by Sarai (1970) that the inclusion of music lessons to the time-table of the school, not only improved the all-round achievement but had acted as a counterweight in relaxing the difficulty of learning scientific subjects. In general, the music education awakened the children's interest towards other arts.

Kodaly — a composer, a folk lorist, a linguist, a teacher, an educator and a patriot of Hungary devised a method of music instruction which has been acclaimed by later investigators to have significant effect on the reading, writing, mathematics and geography achievements of the pupils covered under their studies. Klara Kokas(quoted by Sarai, 1970) using this method observed that music education crossed the boundaries of music itself in its influence and became a more effective means of moulding the individual than could have been expected because the pupil's progress in the school was improved by this technique. There was significant improvement in arithmetic, geography and writing in the experimental group.

Slack (1970) found significant improvement in the skill in all subjects being taught to the students, as a result of music education. He suggested that the level of intelligence of slow-learners can be improved with the addition of music in their general education. In the year 1972, Mills conducted research on the effect of art instruction (music) on the reading development of Appalanchian School in Kansas State of the U.S.A. and observed that the reading can be improved by including music instruction through singing and listening stories with music. Further, he reported that by using a retention test consisting of form II of the WADT (Wepman Auditory Discrimination Test), administered one month later, students, who had received music treatments, performed significantly better than other students who did not. Effect of music listening on correct mathematical responses of 88 Sixth Grade students was studied by Madsen and Forsythe (1973) who found significant differences in mathematical response of the experimental students.

An improvement in the reading response exhibited as correct reading and flash card reading has been reported by Eisenstein (1974) while imparting guitar lessons to slow learners, aged 7 to $7^1/_2$ years. She, further, concluded that music skills activity, demonstrated in a class-room situation is an effective contingency for reading behaviour and possibly for other academic behaviours also. Miller in 1974 conducted a study on 30 educable mentally retarded children in order to study the effect of music listening to either rock music of music classes on arithmetic performance. Significant differences in mathematical responses favouring the experimental groups were found.

The investigator also concluded that the two types of lessons in music did not show significantly variable effects.

Hurwitz and his associates (1975) attempted to measure the sequencing skills and spatial abilities of the language development and readiness in a comparative study of two matched populations. They used the Kodaly method of music instruction : five days per week , 40 minutes per day for seven months and then concluded, that it had significant positive effect on the characteristics they studied, which contributed to the better performance on the MRT (Metropolitan Reading Test) on the experimental children. Their results indicated that there were no significant differences between boys and girls so far as their reading scores and other achievements were concerned.

Attempts to determine the effect of art lessons on the improvement in achievement in mathematics of 667 Fourth Grade children were made by Forseth (1976) using different tests. She found that the experimental group had significant attitude towards mathematics but on the other hand, post-test indicated no significant differences between groups in attitude towards art achievement, achievement in mathematics or creative thinking.

Use of instrumental music has also been tried by some investigators and they found that it had no significant effect. Friedman (1959) compared the two populations of children in Grades IV to VI to assess the effects of instrumental music instruction on their reading and mathematics achievement and found that there were no significant differences between the two groups. The observations made by him were confirmed by Groff(1963) who carried out further work on the same lines in 15 elementary schools in West Harford, Connecticut and his work indicated that there were no significant differences in the academic achievement of children covered under the study, which led him to conclude that withdrawl of pupils to take instrumental music lessons is not deterimental to academic achievement. Helfrich (1973) working in Georgia (U.S.A.) observed that imparting of music in the form of fast or slow music during remedial reading classes to the slow learners showed no significant difference on reading achievements of the experimental and control students of Grade Four. Lauder (1976) found no significant difference between experimental and control groups, comprising of 144 First Grade children, regarding improvement in reading ability with music instructions. The experimental group received music instructions as — i) music exercises correlated with reading tests, ii) activities developed by music specialists to relate music with the reading programme, iii) activities taken from the music tests, and iv) general interest activities.

Music used in the background in a class-room has shown no significant effect as reported by Labach (1960) who studied the effect of background music on reading ability on 476 students of Sixth Grade. Further, four different types of background musics — soft-dreamy, distractive, popular and march, have been tried by Roth (1975) on the reading and comprehensions on 359 High School students from two different schools in Southern Illinois. The students were divided into four groups for the administration of four different types of music to each group. None of the music categories showed any significant effect on the reading ability. However, slight differences did exist but were probably due to individual differences among the students.

In a comprehensive study on 124 First Grade students in Athens (Georgia), Maze (1967) found that there was significant relationship between musicality and verbal reading achievement of the experimental subjects and, he further, observed that this relationship is most pronounced among boys with high musicality profile. He also found significantly high correlation between subjects of the SMMT (Seashore Measure of Musical Talents) and reading achievements. In the year 1968, Jones while studying the relationship between perceptual time span, Intelligence Quotient, music background, and verbal reading achievement on 206 students of various Grades, using various tests like notation, copy test, performance (sight singing), listening test and verbal reading test, observed no significant relationship between verbal reading ability and music reading achievement.

Effect on Adjustment

The remedial measures applied as music education for the control, rather amelioration of behavioural symptoms among the children have been tried by a number of investigators. Normal or mentally handicapped children may show behavioural symptoms which make them maladjusted for the society. With the aim of improving their behavioural traits, various remedial measures like music education, creative art, physical education etc. have been put in use by many investigators in different countries.

Graves (1947) found that adolescents who take music lessons showed less emotional conflict and they appeared to be more comfortable in their relations with their parents than otherwise. Smilansky (1953) working with the mentally retarded children found that there were significant improvements in the adjustment rating and acting out more of their aggression with the help of group play therapy. But there was no difference in the Intelligence Quotient, in general, of the two groups.

Social adjustment of children of Grade III, V, VII, IX and XI totalling 59 students in all, was studied by Hughes (1955) who used rating, socio-grams and California Test of Personality. He concluded that the participation in music education was closely but positively related to social adjustment in school children. Crawford (1961) assessed the effects of art experiences on the self-concept of the institutionalized female mentally retardates, using the Intelligence Quotient scores ranging from 50 to 60. The art classes were held once a week, for ten weeks. He used the Verbal Self Attitude Scale (VSAS) and the Pictorial Test of Self Evaluation (PTSE), both developed by Butler, Guthrie and Gorlow, and concluded that the verbal test provided the evidence that art experiences aided self-adjustment but the PTSE test showed that there was better personal adjustment in the experimental group.

Simpson (1969) studied the effect of school music education on 173 High School students alongwith a control group of 45 and found a positive correlation between the IQ and creative potentials of the experimental group. However, his results were inconclusive to the effect of music on the factors of originality and divergent production of figural system. He suggested that music may be a good stimulant to growth in general creative potentials. Further, he observed that the participation of the students in musical performance in a group tended to be more effective than their individual participation.

Erzsebet, quoted by Sarai (1970) also observed that often singing together with others improved sense of group awareness among the participants than those who did not participate in group singing. Szabo (1970) working in Hungary, reported that singing opens the door to a broader knowledge of music for all. Singing in a group, is an effective means of moulding characters as this evokes feelings of joy, difficult to express in words, feelings of fellowship and the feeling experienced after a successful group performance.

Sokolov (1970) from the U.S.S.R., reported that choir singing which is participation in a group singing, besides helping to breed feelings like patriotism, civic responsibilities and collectivism also helps to strengthen the friendship of world growth. Slack (1970) working in Great Britain, on the slow learners in the schools found that music education helped in the normalization of their pent-up emotions and developed their abilities to the full. Further, Sledzinski in the year 1970, outlined the role of art including music in the life of an individual and found that it shapes integrity, moulds feelings and imagination, induces creative abilities and enables to overcome loneliness, boredom and discouragement.

Klitz (1970) working with population of 619 students including 113 mentally retarded with the I.Q. in the range of 50 to 75 and 106 moderately mentally retarded with an I.Q. range from 30 to 50 under the music education programme which consisted of listening to and participation in the music programme both individual and in groups, observed that many students showed a sense of accomplishment, recognition and achievement in a world where few such opportunities exist for them. He also observed that music, if carefully selected can offer the performer an immediate sense of gratification and accomplishment, to generate enthusiasm, instil confidence and motivate them to seek additional knowledge of music. A number of retardates showed dramatic behavioural changes due to participation in music education programme. This offered pleasurable activities which helped to elevate their morale.

Elord (1972) observed the effects of participation in a combined perceptual-motor and music programme with a music programme, on perceptual motor skill, general behaviour as observed in classroom, personal health habits, physical education, participation and social adjustment. She compared two groups, each of 15 educable mentally retarded children. She concluded that a combined perceptual-motor and music programme developed perceptual-motor skill to much greater degree than the music programme alone, but similar gains were made in social and emotional behaviour in either a combined programme or a programme in music alone.

Wingert (1972) compared 10 mentally retarded children who were involved in music programme of 40 minutes duration, twice a week for eighteen weeks with 10 similar students who did not receive music instruction. The experimental groups showed significant improvement in the basic knowledge, communication, social behaviour and also in measured intelligence. The effect of daily music instruction on the school activities of school students who had never been exposed to music before, has been assessed by Hood (1973) who found that the students having music lessons exhibited better social adjustment than other students. He also made a comparison between the students receiving daily and weekly music lessons and concluded that the students receiving daily music lessons had significant positive effect on personality characteristics and exhibited lower rate of absence from school than did the students of control group.

Music training was found by Kesler (1973) to have little effect on social adjustment of a group of severely and profoundly retarded institutionalized children and adolescents. Further, he found that there was improvement in their music skills.

Maudgalya (1980) found that community singing had a very important role to play at every level of education. Children have a natural aptitude for collective activities. Instead of formal sermon, community singing would be more helpful and successful media for developing a sense of discipline, unity, love and respect for other languages and religion.

Effectiveness of two different approaches of teaching folk songs and popular songs on non-music students has been studied by Douglas (1980) who found no significant differences between the experimental and control groups in areas of cognitive achievement and performance skills but there was a positive significant effect on their attitude towards music.

On the pre and post-test basis, Frank (1981) found improvement both, in quality and quantity of the responses in solving the situational problems by the educable mentally retarded children through music education.

From the available literature, it can be concluded that there is possibility of improvement in the academic achievement and adjustment in the school of the mentally handicapped schools going children. Music education in any form like classical songs, particularly the devotional songs and folk songs or popular songs and National songs can help in their improvement.

Music Therapy through Listening and Participation

Music listening is a wonderful experience. It is an art which involves both the performer and the listener. Both of them are important as far as the psychological effect is concerned. Schopenhauer (1883) acknowledged a connection between human feelings and music, which "restores to us all the emotions of our inmost nature, but entirely without reality and far removed from their pain. Music when presented as an analogue of the emotional life, is a copy or symbol of the will."

According to Copland (1963), Sidney Licht, a Fellow of New York Academy of Medicines, contributed a great deal to the results of research into music therapy and wrote, "I am convinced that listeners are physiologically and psychologically affected by such musical characteristics as mood, intensity, pitch and rhythm and this should provoke remembrance and association of thoughts more easily in a mental patient than methods using factual persuations."

Listening to music has been observed by Copland as an emotional experience or intellectual exercise which depends upon the recptivity and knowledge in music of the listener. Shanti Goverdhan (1957) has described the folk songs as an indicator of the political, social, religious, economic, historical and cultural activities of the area from which they had originated. As such the listener becomes highly involved in it and may start to dance with the tune because it affects the feelings and behaviour of the listener which is likely to bring improvement in the behaviour and achievement of the listener.

Nordoff and Robbins (1965) considered an outstanding contribution of music to the use of music as therapy with handicapped children including the mentally retarded. Their observations were based on work done with 145 children over a considerable period of time. They have been able to delineate 13 categories of responses which described both the "hindrances and malformations" manifested by the children. In working with the responses, the musical experience for the child is affected by the developing and modelling of a particular quality in the therapist's improvisation. This quality may fall into any of the well defined categories of music, or it may be a musical expression that is completely new and belongs only to the particular need of a child. The experience so mediated may be predominantly rhythmic, melodic, harmonic or structural. A very interesting point raised by these workers is that "dynamic, dissonant music does not necessarily excite or disturb psychoitic children". Indeed, this appeared to be a more significant expression for the children than quiet, soothing music, which might be considered more suitable. They established that the "use of improvised music has diagnostic and therapeutic significance." Apparently the technique as employed by Nordoff and Robbins can be extremely helpful in attaining important therapeutic objectives with retardates both on the individual basis and through group musical activities.

Deva (1967) found that a person lacking technical knowledge of music may feel it as emotion; an experienced listener may speak to himself or view the experience as in the strictly descriptive musical terms.

Klitz (1970) reported that music participation helps to increase the power of concentration and attention span, facilitating relaxation, encouraging better posture and proper breathing, improving co-ordination, strengthening specific muscle groups, removing frustration and reducing emotional tension. Teodar Bratu, a Romanian music composer drew attention to the use of local folklore in these songs, stressing that national identity in music for children was important educationally as it acquainted them with the national artistic values handed down the generations : developed the feelings of gratitude and devotion to their country and the working people — the makers of all the material and spiritual values : and helped to raise them in the spirit of humaneness, in a spirit of friendship and respect for all nationals in the world.

Deva (1970) correlated the effect of Indian music on the Indian listener and provided a schematic outline starting from encoder (musician) performing the *Raga* with the emotion and motivation through the frequency, intensity, complexity and modulation of the *Raga* and the *tala* etc. to the decoder (listener) whose auditory perception, emotion and social conditions were observed.

Przychodzinska-Kaciczak (1970), a scientist of Poland working in music, reported that — 1) emotional experience derived from music has an influence on the formation of one's moral and intellectual outlook, 2) music activities develop imagination and creative thinking when confronted with such challenges as to create simple music etc. and 3) contact with music has an influence on the cognitive process, that is, it has the penetrating way of cognizing development of the child's thinking, its role as source of knowledge and deeper understanding of the world, and finally, the significance of music as an element, in mustering humanism.

Direct music participation appears to have a significant positive effect on the development of characteristic of creativity. Sokolov (1970) is of the view that choir singing which is also participation in choir or group singing creates the feelings of patriotism which increases the feelings of pride in one's motherland together with a sense of civic reponsiblity, collectivism and co-operation.

Kaufmann (1979) found that the participation in the recreation of folk songs by young children, have been found to counteract the deleterious effect of passivity in the participants. This increases the aquisition of native language among them and because of simplicity, folk songs are suitable for young children. According to Thanvi (1982), music has limitless effects on human beings since it affects their mental behaviour. Attempts have been made with the help of music to improve the behaviour of the individual from the ancient times. She has further observed that mind is very closely related to music.

Kavanaugh (1982) is of the view that participation in music activities is helpful in the development of vocal concept in children. Music instructions, especially designed for children taking music lessons, help in the development of voice quality, tonal perception and rhythmic equilibrium.

A classical case study on the improvement of a retarded girl through music therapy has been made by G.Orff (1984) who administered the Orff music therapy to Nicole, a six year old girl, who was blind and very seriously retarded in development, as yet incapable of speech herself and with but slight understanding of speech. But she could hear and recall melodies, as was observed from her mimicry and spontaneous hand clapping. Nicole was unable to sit freely, i.e. without support and she was not able to keep hold of mallet given her to play on the mettalophone, it fell out of her hand, at the commencement of the therapy but after fourth session of music therapy, which consisted of 40 minutes music therapy, she was able to retain a grip on the mallet for upto 10 minutes and hammer intensively on the instrument before her. She did so in the manner generally typical for young children that is, pre-melodic and pre-rhymthic. This is impulse playing on a sounding surface and is not precisely responsible in the same sense but out of play grows melodic, rhythmic playing. She had her intonation of various notes. After about eight sessions of music therapy. She could it freely without support, drawn up so to speak by the instrument in front of her and the tones she produced on it.

Music therapy has been found to be very effective in bettering academic achievement and achievements in the school and out of school environment. Listening and participation in the music programmes which may be in any form, i.e. choir or group singing that may include folk songs and other popular songs, is one of the highly effective means of providing music therapy.

Chapter 8

EXPERIMENTAL APPROACH

Since ages, music has been used as an important tool for bringing improvement in an individual or a community so far as the behaviour is concerned. It had been and is still an integral part of our social and cultural life. No ritual or ceremony is complete without music. Even the people who live in the forest or in lonely places, use music as an honourable means of communication. Researchers have been trying to find the reasons for its widespread use in our cultural life but have come to the naked truth that music is and will remain a part of our daily life. Hardly there is any person in the world who does not respond to music, exception is only for deaf or who is severly insane.

Music, in its simplest form is listening to folk songs, popular songs or the beating of drum or playing of flute, has a powerful effect on the human beings. Even the whispering sound of leaves or the murmuring sound of a passerby or chirping sound of birds has effect on the listener. The listener may be passive or active but the effect is there and that effect may be represented sooner or later, depending upon the environment and other conditions. Yet, it is definite that effect of music is certain.

Music education which may be either in the form of listening or participation has been tried by many people of all walks of life for bringing significant improvement in the academic field of students and children of all ages: some of them are Friedman (1959), Groff (1963), Jones (1968), Mills (1972) and Forseth (1976) who found some remarkable effects on the mentally handicapped school going children.

From the available literature, it seems that some work has been conducted in other countries but practically no work has been carried out in India to study the effect of music on the educable mentally children. Therefore, it was proposed to study the effect of music on slow learners.

Objectivbes

The study entitled "Effect of music education on school achievement and adjustment of mentally handicapped children in Himachal Pradesh" was undertaken in Shimla district of the State. The objectives were to observe the effect of music education in the form of listening and participation in the music programmes held or arranged in the class on regular basis, on the school achievement i.e. improvement in the academic field including the subjects of their study like language, general knowledge, social studies, art and mathematics : and school adjustment i.e. improvement in the behaviour and self-adjustment in the school. The other objective was to compare the effect of two types of music — classical, and folk and popular music on the achievement and adjustment in school of the mentally handicapped school going children.

The Approach

In order to achieve these objectives, the research project was carried out on the students of a local school in Shimla town. Since it was not possible to conduct the study on total population so a limited number of individuals from the population were selected. The selected individuals should have all the characters of the population and as such a sample representing the group of the population was selected. This sample was derived out of a school after making a brief survey of all the schools in Shimla town and its adjoining areas with the aim of finding a school where a homogeneous and representative population of 75 students to be put under experimental study could be found, and that should be co-educational, having students from rural and urban areas and of the middle income group. This was done to remove bias in the sample. Thus, the school selected was having students from both the rural and urban backgrounds. It was a co-educational institute where students mostly of the middle class income group were studying. Above all, this school had no provision of music teaching at all. The school was having Hindi as a medium of instruction of their study.

All the students from class VII to X ranging between the age group of 13 to 15 years were taken for the survey work for selection of students to be covered under the present experiment. Total number of students surveyed was 350.

For the determination of their intelligence, students were tested with the Alexander Passalong Test of Intelligence. Students scoring one S.D. below the mean score of their respective age groups were identified as mentally handicapped for the purpose of study. This is based on the work of Herber (1959) and on the basis of the performance of the students, 89 students were identified as mentally handicapped. From this initial pool of 89 mentally handicapped students, only 75 students were selected at random who were the real part of the study. Students under the experiment did not have any auditory impairment. The group of 75 mentally handicapped students were 18 of 13 years age, 30 of 14 years and 27 of 15 years of age. Further, the sample of 75 students was divided into 3 groups of 25 each, by assigning them randomly to each of the group which were — Experimental group A who were given Classical music and Experimental group B were given Folk-popular music and Experimental group C as control and they were not given any music education and were kept busy by their respective teachers.

Three types of tools were used for the conduct of research viz. Psychological tests, Music and Observation schedules. Among the psychological tools, Alexander Passalong Test was employed for measuring intelligence of an individual. The School Adjustment Inventory developed by M.N. Bhagia (1967) was used to study the adjustment to various aspects of school life of the students. This inventory furnished information about the students' adjustment to various aspects of school life in terms of their characteristic behaviour and feelings in and about the school. This inventory had 100 questions, comprising as below :

Area	Number of questions
Adjustment with classroom environment	29
Adjustment with classmates	28
Adjustment with school environment	19
Self-adjustment	24

The questions contained under the area 'Adjustment with Classroom Environment' projected how far a pupil was satisfied with his studies, subjects and classwork; felt confident, serious and successful in school work, and was free from the fear of the tests and examination.

How far a pupil liked his/her classmates; felt happy in their company and enjoyed relationship, experienced approval and popularity among classmates and got into the social interaction by forming friendship and being co-operative was observed under the category of 'Adjustment with Classmates'.

So far as the "Adjustment with School Environment" was concerned, it was judged as to how far a pupil was satisfied with general environment facilities and conformed at school; felt interested and participated in co-curricular activities and experiencesd attachment with the school; liked the teacher of his school, experiences their approval and acceptance, in the class and respectful to them.

From the area of 'Self-Adjustment', the information gathered indicated how far a pupil was satisfied from his "self" at school, felt free from disturbed state of mind, worries, sadness, inadequacies, personal handicaps, immoralities, undue aggressions and conformity, possessed personal qualities like regularity, punctuality, resourcefulness and responsibility.

Music was administered in the form of either Classical music or Folk-Popular music to the mentally handicapped students under the experiment. Classical music being bit difficult for the beginners, its simplest form i.e devotional songs were used. Devotional songs are the easiest for introduction of the Indian Classical music to non-music students. These songs are usually of spiritual themes and they diversify the distraction of the listener. Moreover, these songs are composed in simple tunes which can be sung by children of young age. In all, 12 devotional songs, consisting of *Raga Bhairavi, Asawari, Ahir Bhairav, Bhim Palasi* and *Yaman* were used.

Folk-popular music consisted in rendering the folk songs and popular National songs which are quite popular with the students. Both these types of songs were composed in very popular tunes which can easily be sung by all. Twelve folk songs from the areas of the permanent residence of the students i.e. 3 each from Chamba, Kullu, Kangra and Shimla areas were selected, Seven National songs— *Vande Mataram, Sare Jahan Se Achha Hindustan Hamara, Chalta Chal O Rahi, Honge Kamyab, Yeh Desh Mera Yeh Dhara Meri* and *Barhe Chalo* were also selected as a tool for testing the effect of music education on mentally handicapped students.

Observation Schedules for measuring the extent of achievement and adjustment of the students, three scales viz. Academic Achievement Record, Teachers' Rating and Investigator's Rating were employed. The record collected under 'Academic Achievement Record' provided information regarding the marks obtained by individual student in various subjects of study, during the first Terminal and Annual Examination in the academic session of the school studies. On the basis of marks obtained in different subjects in these two examinations, the improvement or deterioration in subjects of study was worked out.

With the aim of getting information from teachers regarding the behaviour of experimental students in the class and school environment, Teachers' Rating was taken into account. Similarly the effects in terms of changes in the feelings, emotions, moods and other related characters, as a result of music education while the students were listening to, or participating in the music programme being conducted in the classroom, were of great benefit for conducting research in the aspects under study .

The class teachers of respective classes were requested to rate the adjustment of the experimental students in respect to their adjustment with classmates, adjustment with classroom environment, adjustment with school environment and self-adjustment, on the basis of their performance in the classroom and school. They were rated as excellent, good, average, poor and very poor depending upon their response.

Investigator herself scored them excellent, good, average, poor and very poor so far as their interest, patience, involvement, conduct, behaviour and general response during the conduct of music programme was concerned.

Analysis of Data

The results obtained were subjected to statistical interpretation appropriate to the design of Randomised Block Design in the manner as described by Cochran and Cox (1966). The data were tested by F-test at 5 per cent level of significance.

Observations

As a result of the use of music education as a tool for bringing improvement in the school achievement and adjustment of the mentally handicapped children when compared with the control group, there were some marked significant differences.

School Achievement

Effect of the types of music education on the experimental students regarding their achievements in the subjects of their studies was collected as marks obtained in the First Terminal and the Annual Examinations and are disussed as under.

Performances of the two groups receiving music education in the subjects of General Science and Art was significantly better than the control group. In the subject of General Science, there was an average increase of 11.24 and 14.92 per cent obtained by the students of group A and B respectively whereas the control group registered the difference of 6.68 per cent in their means. As far as the subject of Art is concerned, group A receiving Classical music education showed an increase of 9.96 per cent whereas group B receiving Folk-Popular songs showed 11.44 per cent in comparison to group C (5.32 per cent) receiving no music education.

Improvement in Language has been reported by a number of workers like Maze (1967) for First grade students, Mihalyi (1970) for young students, Eisenstein (1974) for students of the age group of 7 to $7^1/_2$ years, and Hurwitz and his associates (1975) for First grade students who found that the reading ability and correct spellings of experimental pupils were improved. The results of the present study are not in conformity with the findings of these investigators. Improvement in reading ability as reported by Maze (1967), Mihalyi(1970), Eisentein (1974) and others were limited to the students of either First grade level or young children whereas the present study has been carried out on VII to IX grade mentally handicapped children which have low intelligence and need more time to understand a particular subject in the class. However, these findings confirm the observations made by Friedman (1959), Labach (1960), Jones (1968), Helfrich (1973), Roth (1975) and Lauder (1976) who found no significant improvement in the subjects of their study.

The significant improvement in the subject of General Science as observed under the present study showed that the students having music education exhibited better performance than students who did not have music education during the course of present investigation. Most of the investigators in the past had limited their studies to Language and Mathematics only and further, their studies were confined to young children who probably did not have this subject in school syllabus.

The subject of Social Studies which included History, Civics and Geography, did not have any significant improvement in the students,. There is a single report by Klara Kokas (1966) which showed that Kodaly method of music education for bringing improvement in the performance in the subject of Geography of the students of young age and average students is good. Music education was a part of school curriculum which might have brought the reported improvement. Under the present study, the scope was limited to mentally handicapped students of the grade levels of VII to IX which was higher than reported by Klara Kokas (1966). Further, the subject of Social Studies is best since it had three subjects including Geography, History and Civics needed more attention span and retention.

As far as the subject of Mathematics was concerned, the results of the present study were different from those obtained by Klara Kokas (1966), Sarai (1970), Madsen and Forsythe (1973) and Miller (1974). According to these investigators, there was some improvement in the performance of students in the subject of Mathematics or Arithmetic. The work of these investigators had been carried out on average students where music education was a part of school education. On the other hand, the results achieved now, which indicated no significant improvement in this subject are inline with the reports of Friedman (1959) and Wolff (1979) who had reported no significant improvement in this subject.

Significant improvement in the performance of experimental groups as a result of music education has been observed under the present study in the subject of Art. Number of investigators had used Art education as a tool for increasing improvement in the achievement of students whereas under this study, the tool — Art, had been used as a variable and effect of music education had been studied on mentally handicapped students in the subject of Art. Improvement in the performance of students having music education may be attributed to the reason that this subject involved the emotions and feelings of the individual for which one is free to express one's ideas and imaginations.

Both these subjects, i.e. Art and Music are inter-related with the emotions and feelings of an individual which seems to have helped the experimental students receiving music education to gain significantly in the subject of Art.

School Adjustment

The adjustment of the mentally handicapped students in the school, tested through School Adjustment Inventory, Teachers Rating and Investigator's Rating was found to be significantly better than the control group. As far as the adjustment of the mentally handicapped students of the experimental groups towards their classroom environment was concerned, it had been observed that the students having music education showed better adjustment than their counterparts who had not received music education. Sledzinski (1970) and Eisenstien (1974) had reported significant improvement in the classroom behaviour of average students as a result of music education. Further, Elord (1972) and Wingert (1972) working with the mentally retarded children had also found significant improvement in their behaviour.

Adjustment with the classmates had been reported to be improved as a result of music education by Erzebet (quoted by Sarai, 1970), Szabo (1970) and Maudgalya (1980) who had observed significant improvement in the adjustment of average experimental students while Elord (1972) and Wingert (1972) had found similar significant effects on the improvement of mentally handicapped students. It had been observed under the present study that the students receiving music education in the form of Classical songs or Folk-Popular songs showed significant improvement in their behaviour towards their classmates as compared to those students who had no music education. Students having music education exhibited better sociability, co-operation and group awareness.

Mentally handicapped students receiving music education in either of the forms employed had exhibited better adjustment with the school environment than others. Scoring on the School Adjustment Inventory and ratings by teachers had indicated that students receiving music education scored higher in their adjustment with the school environments than their counterparts. Earlier Hughes (1955), Sokolov (1970) and Hood (1973) had also reported significant improvement regarding their adjustment with the school environment in the experimental students. Further, Elord (1972) and Wingert (1972) who had carried out research work on the mentally retarded students had found similar effects on them with the help of music education. On the basis of scores obtained by the students receiving music education, it is evident that the results of the present investigation are in line with those of the earlier workers. Experimental students (having music education) took keen interest in school activities like games, sports and other extra-curricular activities in the school. There was also improvement in other characters of the students such as obedience, punctuality and courteousness and behaviour towards their teachers.

So far as self-adjustment in the school by the experimental students is concerned, it has been observed that the students receiving music education had scored significantly higher when tested through School Adjustment Inventory and Teachers' Rating. This indicated that music education in the form of Classical songs or Folk-Popular songs had shown improvement in their behaviour, sociability and confidence in the school. Results on the identical pattern had also been reported by Graves (1947) and Slack (1970) who had found less emotional conflicts among the pupils as a result of music education. Sledzinski (1970) found that music education can overcome loneliness, boredom and discouragement among the students. Development in the personality characters of individuals had been observed by Hood (1973) while Puretz (1973) found better improvement in self-adjustment of the experimental subjects with the music education. Further, significant improvement in the personal behaviour of the children was found to improve as a result of music education (Kesler, 1973). Smilanski (1953), Crawford (1961), Klitz (1970), Elord (1972), Park (1972) and Frank (1981) had found significant improvement as a result of music education or participation in music programmes, in their self-adjustment as shown by increased sense of gratification, confidence, accomplishment, general behaviour and personal habits in the individuals. Under the present study it has been due to the effect of music on the emotions and feelings of the experimental students who had music education in addition to other subjects in their school studies.

According to the ratings made by the investigator herself on the effect of music education on participation and general behaviour of the experimental pupils of the two groups having music education as an additional subject did not show any significant difference in participation and general behaviour of the experimental students during the conduct of music classes.

In general, students having music education had shown better performance than the control group which did not receive music education and these results are in line with the views reported by Deva and Virmani (1968), Altekar (1968), Bhattacharya (1970), Deva (1970), Kaufmann (1979), Thakur (1981) and Thanvi (1982) who had observed significant improvement in the self-adjustment and general behaviour of the individuals as a result of music programme. Mentally handicapped students are usually neglected in the ordinary schools and they suffer from inferiority complex in the school. By providing music education to these students, they might have felt that they have been given some care and attention which helped them to feel themselves better adjusted in the school in various fields of school adjustment. These students also took keen interest and active participation in group singing. Music education provided in any form under the present studies had shown identical effects on school adjustment of the mentally handicapped students.

However, the group which received Folk-Popular songs as music education had exhibited better adjustment in the school than the group receiving music education as Classical songs. This may be due to the reason suggested by Kaufmann (1979) that folk songs being in the native language help in overcoming the deleterious effects of passivity in individuals. Since, the students of the experimental group belonged to rural areas which might have helped them to adjust themselves better to the school environments than other students who did not receive Folk-Popular songs as part of their music education programme.

It may be argued that the changes observed as a result of music education programme in the experimental groups of students are actually due to the factor of attention that was indirectly provided to them by the investigator. But the results obtained in this study are sufficient to negate this argument because the two experimental groups having Classical songs and Folk-Popular songs, which got equal attention from the investigator had shown significant differences in their adjustment with school. In other words, the factor of attention was constant in both the groups. Thus, it can be concluded that significant improvement in adjustment with school among the experimental students as compared to the control group was due to the experimental treatments and not due to the factor of attention. The factor of attention is clearly ruled out as the students of the group which received Folk-Popular songs showed significantly better improvement in school adjustment than the students of the group having Classical songs as music education.

By and large, the results of the present investigation are in full confirmation to point out that both the types of music education whether Classical songs or Folk-Popular songs had exhibited identical effects on the school achievement and school adjustment of the students. Folk-Popular songs had shown significant improvement in the school adjustment of the mentally handicapped students.

Chapter 9

EPILOGUE

Music is the combination of three arts viz. singing, playing of instruments and dancing. The study of the Indian music involves the understanding of its melodic structure and the structure of its rhythm. The chief property of melody, structure of music is the *Nada* or sound. Sound is the sensation caused by certain oscillary motions being transmitted through some medium to the ear. Speech and all the communication of the whole world is dependent on the *Nada*, that is, why it is said that the *Nada* is the supreme power. In music the term *Nada* is used for struck sounds. The *Shruti* or musical sound is the outcome of the *Nada* which is produced through struck sounds. Sound itself is known as the *Shruti* on account of being perceived by the sense of hearing and may be understood as micro-tones. From these micro-tones, which are twenty two in number in the Indian music, emerges the seven principal tones, termed as the *Swara*. The *Swara* means the sound which is the progenitor of the *Raga*. The *Swara* is also known as lit, colour or delight. Scholars of music have defined the *Swara* as the delightful sound. The term *Raga* has been defined as the melodic pattern of tones. A particular sound which is embellished by musical tones and the movement of tonal patterns and is delightful to the people's mind is called the *Raga*.

Music is identified with delight. The element of delight is associated with time. In music, time is a vessal through which tone flows. Time is measured by break up of different accentuations of beats, which creates musical metre. The flow of time is calibrated and this calibration is called the *Laya*. The speed of the rhythm whether slow, medium or fast is measured through the *Tala*. The *Tala* regulates the relative duration of musical sounds. Thus, music has been defined as *''Sawrtala-spadatamkah''* or a composition which is comprised of tone, metre and verse. These elements constitute the sensuous material of music. There is a level of listening on which one simply hears these elements, come and go and responds to them with feelings of pleasantness or unpleasantness.

Music effects the brain through the ears. It first pleases the ears, then stimulates and refreshes the brain with its sweet concord. Rhythm and melody find their way direct to the secret recesses of the soul. Music is the most valuable means which can make a man milder, gentle, better behaved and more reasonable. It eliminates willfulness, impropriety and coarseness from human thoughts and action. On the other hand, it adds firmness, moderation and harmony to the character and leads ultimately to happiness. It strengthens mind and improves concentration through the medium of sweet and beautiful combination of musical notes.

All these qualities of music has paved the way for music therapy. The concept of music therapy is dependent on the correct intonation and right use of the basic elements of music such as the *Nada, Shruti, Swara, Raga, Tala* and *Laya*.

Music is absolutely concerned with the problems of emotional content, value and beauty. It is one of the most wonderful arts in the hands of mankind to alter or modify the feelings and emotions in all living beings to such an extent that it works better than any-other form of therapy in the world. It is the most easiest, cheapest and simplest form of therapy for the correction of many ills and sufferings of the living creatures of this world. A song or a few chords on piano or playing any musical instrument will very quickly change the atmosphere. The effect is both on the performer and the listener. There are number of references and quotations in our books of religion, medicine, culture etc which point out to the fact that music, in any form is a powerful tool in the hands of mankind to bring either goodness or ill-will.

The effect of music therapy may be immediate or slow depending upon a number of factors like the subject, his mental condition, environment and the type of music selected for having the desired effect. Right type of music in its simple and melodic form can calm down even storms but when the loud or harsh music is employed, may provide harmful effects like a peaceful situation may turn into a violent one.

A child is a tender living human being with a highly receptive eager state of mind while both his mind and body are under most active state of development. His mind is just like a clean slate where anything can be written thus, a child has to be brought up in an adequately suitable environment. Now, who is to decide about the environment. It is either the parents or the society who is to create such environment. But in fact, parents are part of society, so it is the duty of our society to provide the children with the most congenial conditions for their development.

A good environment is the one which supplies all the physical materials and moral conditions which stimulate for primary and as well as secondary functions of the individual. Good environment includes the family, school, society and the world around the child which may include flora, fauna and other materials.

Child by nature, may like to do the things by involving his body and brain in such a way that his wishes are fulfilled to the maximum. When these are not fulfilled, he may try to think, imagine and persue his ideas and imaginations to complete his ego. In the normal way, he would be thinking or going towards the creative side but may go otherwise. By getting timely and good help and assistance from his parents, teachers, friends, classmates and others, he may like to improve upon his early ideas. Self-competence, interest, initiatives and alike characters are modified by getting due attention.

Considering the state of intelligence mind of children in general, they may be normal, border-line, mild, moderate, severe and profound, apart from the gifted ones. There is no problem for the normal or average, border-line, and gifted children as far as their improvement is concerned but others need some care. They are generally regarded as mentally handicapped, mentally retarded, or educable mentally retardates or simply retardates. These children look like the normal children in all physical appearances. Their way of doing the things, and general habits are like the normal ones. They do have the same needs like food, clothing, aesthetic needs, physical urges, existence and other requirements like the normal children except that they are slow in doing the things and in learning. But when they are neglected or they feel neglected, their problem starts. Generally, at this age, the mentally handicapped children are old enough to feel ashamed and they may resent of being isolated or being transferred to places where only mentally handicapped children are kept and they do not like to be put under special institutions. Now, at this stage, these children often become troublesome for parents and teachers.

It is the foremost duty to identify such children that may seem to be slow learners or lacking behind other children in a class or in a group. The idea is to find out the extent to which they are lagging behind, most of the mentally handicapped i.e. slow learners can cope up with this situation. These children may need special or extra classes and attention which requires the genuine attempts to provide the education/training suitable to their requirements.

It is the quality of a good teacher or a trainer to provide such type of training and attention that these children are accepted by their classmates and the society.

At this juncture, music plays a pivotal role in moulding the personality and behaviours of such children. Since by definition and tradition, music which is melodious or harmonious is known as music. The melodic effect of music is due to variation in the sound waves which is pleasant to the ears and thus, may passify the aggressive and repulsive behaviour of the mentally handicapped.

Experiments have been conducted in India and abroad to find out the effect of music on the mentally handicapped children. Though much work has been carried out in foreign countries which goes in favour of suggesting in depth study into the effect of music on scientific basis. Case studies too have been carried out, under which special attention has been provided to the child which may be direct or indirect but when they are treated in group, they get the feeling of company and then there arises the spirit of competition which helps all the children to get themselves improved and this results in a positive effect of music.

This type of education or training depends upon not only on the policy and organization but on the human qualities of the teacher. A good music programme involves a good and efficient music teacher.

A god music educator who has a basic concept of social psychology or is acquainted with the fundamentals and principles of behavioural changes, can perform the duties of a good musico therapist. A skillful and a patient teacher can do good work even in a bad situation or system while an arrogant and quick tempered teacher may render all the available opportunities ineffective or useless for these children. Society should help such teachers by creating amiable conditions for such type of education. This is by gaining co-operation from all quarters i.e. organizations, children, parents and other colleagues in creating suitable environment and better atmosphere.

Music is not merely a subject of study limited to the four walls of a classroom or to the *Guru-shishya Parampara* (teacher taught traditional system) but is a subject of helping the mankind to improve their lot by incorporating all sorts of knowledge and experience for attainment of good human beings.

Apart from the sound knowledge of the music, a teacher must have some other qualities like thinking ability, imagination, inspiration, expression of emotions and feelings, balanced mood, intelligence, ability to compose the music and the style of its presentation.

Similarly, the listener or the subject must have the power and capacity to perceive, intelligence, emotionality, receptivity, memory and learning ability. Mentally handicapped children are slightly different from the normal children since they have low Intelligence Quotient (I Q) and they need care and attention from all quarters of society including the parents. All other branches of knowledge are not as effective as the music itself since the effect of music in different forms on every aspect of human life as well as the plants and animals, is supreme. Its physiological, psychological, physical, prenatal and moral effects on human beings have been fully established which point to the fact that music has a dynamic power on the behavioural changes in a living being. This testifies the use of music as a therapeutic tool in curing a number of diseases like hypertension, depression, aggressiveness, arthiritis, rheumatism, stomach disorders, mental weakness, insomania, malaria, hysteria, tuberculosis, typhoid, constipation etc. Indian classical music has been found to be very beneficial in this respect in comparison to the Western music.

Music-therapy is going to be very relevant in the coming future due to the costly treatment through medicines beyond the reach of common man. Moreover, medicines may have many side effects from which music therapy is free.

Attempts have been made in India to use the Indian classical music as a therapeutic agent by various workers. Some studies have been conducted to observe the effect of music education on the mentally handicapped children on their general achievement in their studies and academic career and their adjustment in society, school and environment. The use of folk or popular music has been found to be effective in this direction. Listening to and participation in music activities increased their level of intelligence, concentration, attention span and academic achievement. Similarly, improvement in their general behaviour, adjustment in society and home has also been reported by many researchers.

Bimalendu Mukherjee has invented a *Raga-Anandmayee* for the cure of hypertension and like diseases which has met with great success due to the fact that the effect is not by gimmic but is due to the effect of music reaching to the soul of the listener or the patient in creating right type of emotions and feelings.

Such findings have inspired the educationists, psychologists, psychiatrists and music therapists to use music as or in therapy for the amelioration of the mentally handicapped children. Thus, they designed special education for them. Recreational services, art activities, physical education, occupational therapy, leisure education, psychotherapy, play therapy, extra-curricular activities are among the adjunctive therapies which are being introduced as special education for this strata of society.

Imparting music education and using music as or in therapy points to a tradition that the slow-learners are permitted and encouraged to participate in extra-curricular, aesthetic and atheletic activities on the same basis as other normal students.

In this age of technological advancement, it is now possible to measure the effects of music with suitable instruments and other gadgets. Elector-encephelograph can be used to produce an 'autonomic diagram'. With the help of this instrument, assessment of amplitude and frequency of the brain waves can be measured and with the use of electro-cardiograph, action on heart rhythms can be recorded. Similarly, a spirometer can be used to record the rate and depth of respiration. An oscillograph can be used for the interpretation of sound waves and a plenthysmograph for the interpretation of blood flow conditions. A psychogalvanic skin reflex recorder can be an helpful instrument for recording skin reflexes and an electromyograph to study the myopic conditions of the eyes while using music in or as therapy.

All these instruments are of immense help in the standardization of the type of music being used to cure different types of diseases and ailments and to boost the measures taken for the amelioration of the mentally handicapped children. It will then surely prove the saying—

'Give them the opportunity to prove their ability'

LITERATURE CITED

Ahobal, 1956. Sangit Parijat, Sangit Karyalaya, Hathras.

Atlekar, M.V. 1968. "(Sangit Dwara Rogopachar). "Sangeet, 34(4): 24-25,68.

Atri, Sitaram. 1981. "(Sangit Ka Manovigyan)." Sangeet, 47 (3): 26-38.

Baumeister, A. A. 1967. Mental Retardation, Appraisal, Education and Rehabilitaion. University of London Press, London.

Bhagia, M. N. 1967. The School Adjustment Inventory. Manasayan, 32 Netaji Subhash Marg, Delhi.

Bhatia, H. R. 1977. A Textbook of Educational Psychology. The McMillan Company of India Ltd. Delhi.

Bhattacharya, S. 1970. "(Mansik Rogon Ke Liye Sangit Chikitsa)." Sangeet, 36(10-11) : 7.

Bratu, T. 1970. Actual problems of musical creativity for children. Report presented at Composers' Roundtable Session, International Society for Music Education In Music Education in Modern World. 1974, Progress Publishers, Moscow, 1974. p. 165.

Burt, C. 1969. The Backward Child. University of London Press, London.

Chawla, P. L. and J. S. Neki. 1978. "Mental retardation- A study of parent's 'appreciative abililty' and experiences." Jour. All India Inst. Med. Sciences, 3(1) : 87-96.

Cochran, W. G. and G. M. Cox. 1966. Experimental Design. John Wiley and Sons Ltd., New York, London, Sydney. 95-105.

Copland, A. 1952. Music and Imagination. C.E. Norton Lectures, Harward.

Copland, A. 1963. Copland on Music. "Pyramid Books. New York.

Crawford, J. W. 1961. The effect of art experience on the self-concept of institutionalised adolescent female mental retardates, Pennsylvania. Ed.D. Dissertation, The Pennsylvania State University, Diss. Abst., 22: 3919 - A.

Davis, M. 1965. Implications of finger painting for the child with retarded mental development. Recreation for the Ill and Handicapped. 9 : 5-6.

DeMartino, M. F. 1957. Some observations, concerning psychotherapeutic techniques with the mentally retarded. In Councilling and Psychotherapy with the Mentally Retarded. (Eds. Stacey C.L. and M.F. DeMartino), Glencoe, Illinois Free Press, 461-472.

Desai, H. J. M. 1981. "What needs to be done ?" Illustrated Weekly of India, Dec. 13-18, 22-23.

Deva, B. C. 1967. Psychoacostics of Music and Speech. The Music Academy, Madras.

Deva, B. C. 1970. "Some problems in science and music: Exploration in possibilities". Sangeet Natak, 16:15-22.

Deva, B. C. and K. G. Virmani. 1968. "Meaning of music : An empirical study of psychological responses to Indian Music." Sangeet Natak, 10: 54-93.

Doghlas, T. S. 1980. The comparative effectiveness of two methods of teaching fundamentals of music: A Gestalt centred approach using popular and folk songs and a more traditional approach using folk songs and children songs. D.M.A. University of Southern California, Diss. Abst. Inter. 41(6) : 2490 - A.

Eisentein, S. R. 1974. "Effect of contingent guitar lessons on reading behaviour." Jour. Music Therapy, XI (3) : 138-146.

Elord, J. M. 1972. The effects of perceptual-motor training and music on perceptual-motor development of educable mentally retarded children. Ed. D. Dissertation, The Lousiana State University and Agricultural and Mechanical College. Diss. Abst. Inter., 33: 2148 - A.

Enderson, E. 1952. Plants, Man and Life. Berkley University, California Press.

Farnsworth, P. 1967. Review. J. A. A. C. 26(1) : 142.

Feser, G. 1984. Musicotherapy, Principles and Potentials; Medical Focus, 2 : 84. 12-16.

Flaherty, Vera. 1956. "History and development of occupational therapy." Amer. Jour. Mental Deficiency, 60: 755-759.

Forseth, S.D. 1976. The effects of art activities on attitudes and achievement in Fouth-Grade children pertinent to the learning of mathematics and art. Ph.D. Dissertation, University of Minnisota, Diss. Abst. Inter. 37: 7590 - A.

Frank, H.R. 1981. The influence of training upon the educable mentally retarded child's situational problem solving ability. Diss. Abst. Inter. 42(5): 2070 - A.

Freeman, M. 1956. "Drawing as a psychotherapeutic intermedium." Amer. Jour. Mental Deficiency, 60 : 755-759.

Friedman, B. 1959. An evaluation of the achievement in reading and arithmatic of pupils in Elementary School instrumental music classes. Ed. D. Dissertation, New York University, Diss. Abst. Inter. 20 : 120.

Gangrade, K.D. 1989. Community Organization and Delivery of Health Service in Rural India. In Disabilities and Impairments. 3(1): 1-14.

Gaston, E.T. 1968. Music in Therapy. MacMillan, New York.

Goswami, R. 1977. "(Man Aur Sangit.)" Sangeet, 43(5): 26-27.

Goswami, R. 1977a. "(Bhavabhivyakti Evam Sangit Ke Dwara Iski Poorti)." Sangeet, 43(7): 15-16.

Graves, W.S. 1947. "Factors associated with children taking music lessons, including some parent-child relationships." Ped. Sem. 70:65-125.

Groff, F.H. 1963. Effect on academic achievement of excusing elementary school pupils from classes to study instrumental music. Ph.D. Dissertation, The University of Connecticut. Diss, Abst. 25:5014.

Gupta, S.C. and B.B. Sethi. 1970. "Prevalence of mental retardation in Uttar Pradesh." Ind. Jour. Psychology, 12:264.

Hadley, J.M. 1958. Clinical and Counselling Psychology. Alfred A Knopf. New York.

Hanshumaker, J. 1980. "The effects of arts education on intellectual and social development: A review of selected research." Council for Research in Music Education, Bull. 61, 10-28.

Heck, A.O. 1953. The Education of Exceptional Children. McGraw Hill Book Co., Inc. New York.

Heimlich, E.P. 1960. Music as therapy with emotionally disturbed children. Child Welfare, 39: 3-7.

Helfrich, D.C. 1973. The effect of rock music, controlled for tempo and volume on disabled readers in remedial reading classes. Ph.D. Dissertation. University of Georgia, Diss. Abst. Inter. 34:3024 - A.

Herber, R. 1959. "A manual on terminology and classification in mental retardation." Amer Jour. Mental Deficiency, Monograph Supplement, 64.

Herber, R. 1961. "Modification in the manual on terminology and classification in mental retardation." Amer. Jour. Mental Deficiency, 65 (4) : 499-500.

Hoffmann, K. 1970. "Further development of the music education curricula in the G.D.R. — An important means of securing a high level of music education."

Paper read at the Special Session of IX Conference of International Society for Music Education. In Music Education in the Modern World, 1974. Progress Publishers, Moscow. 1974. 242-244.

Hood, B.S.III. 1973. The effect of daily instruction in public school music and related experiences upon non-musical personal and school attitudes of average achieving Third Grade students. Ed.D.Dissertation, Mississipi State University, Diss. Abst. Inter. 34:4880 - A.

Hughes, Jo. Ann M. 1955. "Fifty nine case studies on the effect of musical participation on social development." Music Educators Journal, 41 (Feb.), 58-59.

Hurwitz, I. and Associates. 1975. "Non-musical effects of the Kodaly music curriculum in Primary-Grade children." Journal of Learning Disabilities, VIII (March) : 167-174.

Hutt, M.L. and R.C. Gibby. 1958. The Mentally Retarded Child : Development, Education and Guidance. Allyn and Becon. Boston.

International Folk Music Council Year Book. 1969. Quoted from the New Encyclopaedia Britannica, Knowledge in Depth, Vol. VI, 1973-74, University of Chicago, U.S.A.

Itard, J.M.G. 1801. The Wild Boy of Aveyron. Translated by G.M. Humphrey (1932), Appleton - Century Groffs. Inc. New York.

Johnson, G.O. 1963. Education for the Slow Learners. Prentice Hall Inc., Englewood Cliff, N.J.

Jones, H.T. Jr. 1968. The relationship of selected factors and music reading achievement. Ph.D. Dissertation, Michighan State University, Diss. Abst. Inter. 2: 3632 - A.

Jordan, A.M. 1953. Measurement in Education: Measurement of Fine Arts and Manual Arts. McGraw Hill Book Co., Inc.

Joseph, H. and E.P.Heimlich. (1959) "The therapeutic use of music with 'treatment resistant' children." Amer. Jour. Mental Deficiency. 64 : 41-49.

Kadis, A.L. 1957. The use of finger painting in psychotherapy with mentally retarded children. In Counselling and Psychotherapy with the Mentally Retarded (Eds. Stacey, C.L. and M.F. DeMartino) Glencoe, Illinois, Free Press. 255-258.

Kaufmann, S. 1979. Aesthetic development of young children through folk songs. Ph.D. Dissertation, New York University, Diss. Abst. Inter. 40(11) : 5773 - A.

Kavanaugh J.M. 1983. The development of vocal concept in children: The methodologies recommended in designated elementary music series. Ph.D. Dissertation, North Texas State University, 1982. Inter. Diss. Abst. 43(7): 2270-A.

Keeley, K. 1962. "Prenatal influences on behaviour of offspring of crowded mice." Science, 135: 44.

Kesler, E.B.Jr. 1973. The effect of a music training program on the music production skills: Social development of severely retarded institutionalized children and adolescent. Ed. D. Dissertation, University of Georgia, Diss. Abst. Inter. 43: 3991 - A.

King, F.W. 1954. "The use of drawings of human figure as an adjunct in psychotherapy." Jour. Clinical Psychology, 10: 65-69.

Kirk, S.A. 1970. Educating Exceptional Children. Oxford and I B H Publishing Co., Bombay.

Klitz, B. 1970. "The role of music in the life of the mentally retarded at Mansfield Training School." Paper read at the Special Session of IX Conference of International Society for Music Education. In Music Education in the Modern World. 1974. Progress Publishers, Moscow. 1974. 324-326.

Kraus, R.G. 1943. Mental Illness and Mental Retardation. MacMillan Co., New York.

Labach, J.P. 1960. The effects of background music on reading comprehension and their relationship to various other characteristics in Sixth-Grade students. Ph.D. Dissertation, Syracuse University, Diss. Abst. Inter. 21:350.

Lauder, D.C. 1976. An experimental study of the effect of musical activities upon reading achievement of First-Grade students. Ed. D. Dissertation, University of South Carolina, Diss. Abst. Inter. 37:1975 - A.

Lawrence, Ian. 1978. Composers and the Nature of Music Education. Scolar Press, London.

Leonard, C. and R.W. House. 1959. Foundations and Principles of Music Education. McGraw Hill Publishers, New York.

Leslie, L.H. 1981. A comparison of the effects of a 9 - month educational program versus a 12 - month educational program on academic achievement and adaptive behaviour of three groups of retarded students in residential and community settings. Ph.D. Dissertation, University of Mississippi, Diss. Abst.Inter. 42:7, 3107 - A.

Madhuvrat Madhugandha. 1993. "(Rag chikista)". Sangeet. 59(12) : 23-29.

Madsen, C.K. and J.L. Forsythe. 1973. "Effect of contingent music listening on increases of mathematical responses." Jour. Res. Music Education. XXI, Summer, 176-181.

Maslow, A.H. 1954. Motivation and Personality. Harper and Co. New York.

Matang Muni. Brihaddeshi. Sangit Karyalaya. Hathras.

Maudgalya, V.C. 1980. Music For All. In 3rd Chandigarh Sangit Sammelan, Indian National Theatre, Chandigarh.

Maze, N.M. 1967. A study of the correlations between musicality and reading achievement of First-Grade level in Athens, Georgia. Ed.D. Dissertation, Uni. of Georgia, Diss. Abst.Inter. 28 : 3895 - A.

Menuhin, Yehudi and C.W. Davis. 1980. The Music of Man. MacDonald and Jones Publishers Limited. London.

Michel, P. 1970. Music education in the G D R as a means of an all-round and harmonious development of personality. Report made at Plenary Session of IX Conf. Inter. Soc. for Music Education. In Music Education in the Modern World, Progress Publishers, Moscow. 1974, 83-86.

Mihalyi, G. 1970. Development of reading, writing and counting skills in seven-year-old pupils in general schools with music education. Paper read at the Special Session of IX Conference of International Society for Music Education. In Music Education in the Modern World. Progress Publishers, Moscow. 1974. 260-262.

Miller, D.M. 1974. Effects of selected music listening contingencies on arithmetic performance and music performance of educable mentally retarded children. Ed. D. Dissertation, Columbia University, Diss. Abst. Inter. 35:3555 - A.

Mills, J.C. 1972. The effect of art instruction upon a reading development test: An experimental study. Ph.D. Dissertation, University of Kansas, Diss. Abst. Inter. 33: 6596 - A.

Mohan, J.K. and R. Bajaj. 1983. A study of vigilance of Gifted, Normal and Mentally Retarded Children. IX All India Congress on Mental Retardation, Sagar.

Mohan, J.K. and S. Bhatia. 1985. "Psychomotor performance of mentally retarded, normal and gifted children". Disability and Impairment, Vol. 3(1).

Mohan, J.K. and M.Jain. 1979. "A study of choice reaction time as a function of intelligence". Journal of Social Science Research. 4(3) : 55-61.

Mukherjee, Bishwanath. 1956. Alexander Passalong Test: Direction for Administration and Scoring. Phy-schologist. B M Institute of Psychology and Child Development, Ahmedabad.

Muller, Z.P.L. 1982. A historical and comparative study of role of music in child education. D.Ed. Dissertation, University of Pretoria, Diss Abst. Inter. 44(6) : 1720 - A.

Mursell, J.L. 1937. The Psychology of Music. W.W. Norton and Company Inc. New York.

Narayanan, H.S. 1981. "A study of the prevalence of mental retardation in Southern India". Inter. Jour. Mental Health. 10,28.

Nketia, J.H.K. 1961. The Preservation of Traditional Forms of the Learned Music of the Orient and the Occident. International Music Council, Paris, 203-213.

Nordoff, P. and C. Robinsons. 1965. Music Therapy for Handicapped Children: Investigations and Experi-ences. Rudolph Steiner Publications. Blauvelt, N.Y.

Omcheri, Leela and O.D. Bhalla. 1990. Studies in Indian Music and Allied Arts. Sandeep Prakashan. Delhi.

Orff, G. 1984. "Orff Music Therapy." Medical Focus. 2/84: 18.

Park, K. 1972. Relationship between self-concept and achievement in a moderately mentally retarded population. Ed.D. Dissertation, University of Cincinati, Diss. Abst.Inter. 40:9, 3956 - A.

Pathak, S. 1969."(Swasthya par Sangit Ka Prabhav.)" Sangeet, 35(12), 30-32.

Pruetz, S.L. 1973. A comparison of the effects of dance and physical education on the self-concept of selected disadvantaged girls. Ed.D. Dissertation, New York University, Diss. Abst. Inter. 34:3124 - A.

Przychodzinska- Kaciczak. 1970. Modern trends in music education in Polish secondary schools. Paper read at the Special Session of IX Conference of International Society for Music Education, In Music Education for the Modern World, Progress Publishers, Moscow. 1974. 295-298.

Rice, G.H. 1979. A Hindustan Binet Performance Scale, Oxford University Press, Bombay.

Robinson, H.B. and N.M. Robinson. 1965. The Mentally Retarded Child: A Psychological Approach. McGraw Hill, New York.

Roth, C.F. Jr. 1975. The effects of background music on knowledge, comprehension, application and analysis types of learning . Ph.D. Dissertation, South Illinois University, Diss. Abst. Inter. 36:7751 - A.

Sarai, T. 1970. The role of music in the life of children and young people. Report made at the Plennary Session of the IX Conference of International Society for Music Education. In Music Education in the Modern World, Progress Publisihers, Moscow. 1974. 119-130

Schenider, H.E. 1956."Relationships between musical experiences and certain aspects of cerebral palasied children's performance on selected tasks." Journal of Music Therapy. 250-277.

Schlotter, B.E. and M.Svendsen. 1959. An Experiment in Recreation with Mentally Retarded. Department of Public Welfare. Springfield, Illinois.

Schopenhaure, A. 1883. (Die Welt als Wille and Vorstellung) Quoted from the New Encyclopaedia Britanica, Knowledge in Depth, Vol. IX, University of Chicago, 1973-74.

Shanti Goverdhan, 1957. Sangit Shastra Darpan Part II, Prayag Sangeet Samiti, Allahabad. 66-67.

Sharangdev. 1896. Sangit Ratnakar. Anand Mundranalaya, Bombay.

Shirali, V.D. 1977. Sargam : An Introduction to Indian Music. Abhinav Publications. New Delhi.

Simpson, D.J. 1969. The effect of selected musical studies on growth in general creative potential. Ed. D. Dissertation, University of California, Diss. Abst. Inter. 30:502 - A.

Sinclair, S. 1979. National Planning for the Mentally Handicapped. Report of the Expert Group on National Planning for the Mentally Handicapped in India. Sponsored by the Director-General of Health Services, W H P and the All India Institute of Medical Sciences, New Delhi.

Singh, M.V. and B. Dagar. 1982." Sociological aspects of behaviour problems in a community child guidance centre". Child Psychiatry Quarterly. 15(2): 43-49.

Slack, R. 1970. The role of music in the lives of children and young people. Paper read at the Special Session of IX Conference of International Society for Music Education. In Music Education in the Modern World, Progress Publishers, Moscow. 1974. 252-255.

Sledzinski, S. 1970. Music in the life of the new generation of the Polish People's Republic. Report made at the Plennary Session of IX Conference of International Society for Music Education. In Music Education in the Modern World, Progress Publishers, Moscow. 1974. 135-140.

Smilansky, S. 1953. Possible approaches of applying group psychothreapy to institutionalized mentally retarded children. Doctor's Thesis. Ohio State University.

Sokolov, V. 1970. Choir singing as a means of cultivating a sense of patriotism, civic responsibility and collectivism in a community of children and young persons. Paper read at the Special Session of IX Conference of International Society for Music Education. In Music Education in the Modern World. Progress Publishers, Moscow. 1974. 364-366.

Subramanya, B. 1983. An epidemiological study of mental retardation in rural children. M.D. Thesis. University of Bangalore.

Swanson, R.B. 1961. Music in the Education of Children. Wadsworth, San Francisco.

Szabo, H. 1970. The development of team spirit through ensemble music-making in senior classes of general education schools with music tution. Paper read at the Special Session of IX Conference of International Society for Music Education. In Music Education in the Modern World. Progress Publishers, Moscow. 1974. 265-266.

Terman. L.M. 1916. The Measurement of Intelligence. Houghton Mifflin Company. Boston.

Thakur, V.S. 1981. "(Sangit ka Chamatkar)." Sangeet. 47(4): 45-47, 57.

Thambe, Balaji. 1994. Music Therapy, The Tribune, Oct., 14, 7.

Thanvi, P. 1982. "(Mansik Aswasthya Aur Sangitik Upchar)". Sangeet. 48:5. 5-11.

Tiwari, R. 1980. "(Pandit Onkar Nath Thakur ke Chamatkarik Sangit Anubhav.)" Sangeet. 46:12, 21-22, 27.

W.H.O. 1959."Organisations of Services for the Mentally Retarded. Technical Report Series No. 392.

Wallace, W.J.E. Education of Mentally Handicapped Children. Harper and Brothers, New York.

Weigh, V. 1959. "Functional music, a therapeurtic tool in working with the mentally retarded." Amer.Jour. Mental Deficiency. 63:672-678.

William, G. 1975. "Helping the handicapped, science reaches for miracles". Family Health. 7, 26.

Wingert, M.L. 1972. "Effects of a music enrichment program in the education of the mentally retarded." Jour. Music Therapy. IX, Spring, 13-22.

Wolff, K.L. 1979. The effects of general music education on the academic achievement, creative thinking and school attendance of First Grade children. Ph. D. Dissertation. University of Michighan. Diss. Abst. Inter. 40:10. 5359 - A.

List of Hindi Words with English Appropriates

Hindi	English
Agni	Fire, energy
Ahata	Struck sound
Anahata	Unstruck sound
Ananda	Pleasure
Anuddatta	Vedic musical notes lower
pitch	
Ashtavakra	A character in Mahabharata who had eight deformities in the body
Atharveda	Fourth Veda
Atisukshama	Very minute
Ativyakta	highly expressed
Audava	Having Five notes
Ayurveda	Science of medicines
Brahma	God of C
Bhaishaj	Medicine
Bhaishaj-tatva	Medicinal elements
Bhayanaka	Dreadful
Bheri	Percussion instrument
Chakra	Circle
Chakravyuha	A special type of army formation in circles
Charak	Pioneer of Ayurvedic System of medicines
Chitt	Mind
Dharma	Religion
Gayan vidhan	Style of singing
Geet	Song

Graha	Planets
Gram-raga	A classification of ragas
Hanumana	A God
Jati raga	A classification of ragas
Kala	Time
Kapha	Cough
Karma	Deed
Kirtan	Religious Song
Komal	Flat note
Krishna	A God
Kritrima	False, artificial
Laya	Beat of time, tempo
Layakari	Different types of rhythm
Madhya	Middle octave
Mandra	Lower octave
Manjeera	A struck instrument
Moksha	Salvation
Mridanga	A percussion instrument
Nada	Sound
Nada-brahma	Divine sound
Narada	A Saint
Nritya	Dance
Pada	Verse
Panava	A percussion instrument
Parvati	A Goddess
Pitt	Disorder caused by bodily scretions
Prana	Soul

Raga	Melody
Raga-dhyana	Iconography of ragas
Rajasa	Kingly
Rigveda	First Veda
Rishi	Saint
Sadhana	Practice
Samaveda	3rd Veda
Sampurna	Having seven notes
Complete	
Sangit	Music
Sannipata	Delirium
Saral gati	Easy movement
Saraswati	Goddess of learning
Satva	Truth
Shabda	Words
Shabda-brahma	Lord of knowledge
Shadava	Having six notes
Shakti	Goddess of power
Shankha	A wind instrument
Shiva	God
Shruti	Micro-tones
Shudha	Pure, Natural musical notes
Sthana	Octave
Sukshma	Minor, minute
Sushruta	Pioneer of yurvedic medicines
Swara	Musical notes
Swaritt	Drone, Vedic notes
Tala	Rhythm cycle
Tamasa	Darkness
Tantari	A string instrument
Thata	Originator of raga (melody)
Tivra	Sharp notes

Udatta	Vedic notes, high pitch
Vadya	Instruments
Vaka	Speech
Vekra gati	Obstacled movement
Vansh	A wind instrument
Vat	Bodily disorder caused by wind
Vedanta	Knowledge about Vedas
Vedic	Pertaining to Veda
Veena	A string instruments
Venu	A wind instruments
Vibhatsa	Very ugly
Vikrita	Modulation of notes
Vilambita	Slow rhythm
Vishnu	A God
Vyakta	Expressed
Yoga	Yoga
Yogi	A person practising yoga

INDEX

N

O

P

R

S